STANDARDS FOR THE PROFESSIONAL PRACTICE OF INTERNAL AUDITING

Statements on Internal Auditing Standards Nos. 1-18

Statement of Responsibilities of Internal Auditing

Code of Ethics

THE INSTITUTE OF INTERNAL AUDITORS
249 Maitland Avenue
Altamonte Springs, Florida 32701-4201

The Institute of Internal Auditors is an international association dedicated to the continuing professional development of the individual internal auditor and the internal auditing profession.

Procedures for obtaining permission to translate or adapt any part of this document are included on pages 113 through 115.

To obtain permission to translate, adapt, or reproduce any part of this document, contact:

>Lucy Sheets, Coordinator
>The Practices Center
>The Institute of Internal Auditors
>249 Maitland Avenue
>Altamonte Springs, Florida 32701-4201
>Phone: (407) 830-7600, ext. 256
>FAX: (407) 831-5171

ISBN 0-89413-400-0

99241 10/99

Contents

Foreword

This volume, issued by the Practices Center of The Institute of Internal Auditors (IIA), represents the fifth codification of the *Standards for the Professional Practice of Internal Auditing (Standards)* and *Statements on Internal Auditing Standards (SIAS)*.

As internal auditing adapted to the continuous changes in organizations and in society, the guidelines contained in the *Standards* have been modified by the issuance of *SIASs*. *SIASs* are issued by the Internal Auditing Standards Board, the technical committee of The IIA responsible for promulgating and monitoring the *Standards* and other Standards Pronouncements on a worldwide basis.

Standards, as used in this document, means the criteria by which the operations of an internal auditing department are evaluated and measured. They are intended to represent the practice of internal auditing as it should be. The *Standards* are meant to serve the entire profession in all types of organizations where internal auditors are found.

The following is an overview of the *SIASs* appearing in this codification:

1. *SIAS No. 1* — **Control: Concepts and Responsibilities**
   This SIAS has been codified into original Guidelines 300.02, subsections .1-.7; 300.03, subsections .1-.2d. Additional Guidelines 300.06, subsections .1-.4; 300.07, subsections .1-.4 and 300.08, subsections .1-.3 have been added.
   The Background section of *SIAS No. 1* has not been codified.
   (Issued July 1983.)

2. *SIAS No. 2* — **Communicating Results**
   This SIAS has been codified into original Guidelines 430.01, subsections .1-.2; 430.02, subsections .1-.2; 430.03, subsec-

tions .1-.5; 430.04, subsections .1-.8; 430.05, subsections .1-.2; 430.06, subsection .1; 430.07, subsections .1-.3.
(Issued July 1983.)

3. **SIAS No. 3 — Deterrence, Detection, Investigation, and Reporting of Fraud**
This SIAS has been codified into original Guidelines 280.01, subsections .1-.5g; 280.02, subsections .1-.3; 280.03, subsections .1-.6d.
(Issued May 1985.)

4. **SIAS No. 4 — Quality Assurance**
This SIAS has been codified into original Guidelines 560.01, subsections .1-.4g; 560.02, subsections .1-.3; 560.03, subsections .1-.6; 560.04, subsections .1-.7.
Two paragraphs of *SIAS No. 4* which originally appeared as paragraphs 560.03.7 and 560.04.8 have been omitted.
(Issued November 1986.)

5. **SIAS No. 5 — Internal Auditors' Relationships with Independent Outside Auditors**
This SIAS has been codified into original Guidelines 550.01, subsections .1-.6; 550.02, subsections .1-.4d.
Additionally, the term "independent outside auditor" has been changed to reflect the original terminology "External Auditor." Also, the Background section of *SIAS No. 5* has been omitted.
(Issued June 1987.)

6. **SIAS No. 6 — Audit Working Papers**
This SIAS has been codified into original Guidelines 420.01, subsections .5a-.5s.
(Issued December 1987.)

7. **SIAS No. 7 — Communication with the Board of Directors**
This SIAS has been codified into original Guidelines 110.01, subsections .2a, .4a, .5a-d, .6a-e; 550.01, subsections .7-.8.
(Issued June 1989.)

8. **SIAS No. 8 — Analytical Auditing Procedures**
This SIAS has been codified into original Guidelines 420.01, subsections .1a-.1n.
Additionally, Guideline 420.01.1a has been added to serve as an introduction to the material codified in *SIAS No. 8.*
(Issued December 1991.)

9. **SIAS No. 9 — Risk Assessment**
This SIAS has been codified into original Guidelines 520.04, subsections .1-.14.
Additionally, Guidelines 520.04.1 and 520.04.14 have been added to the material codified in *SIAS No. 9.* Also, the Background section of *SIAS No. 9* has been omitted.
(Issued December 1991.)

10. **SIAS No. 10 — Evaluating the Accomplishment of Established Objectives and Goals for Operations or Programs**
This SIAS has been codified into original Guideline 350.01, subsections .1-.9.
(Issued December 1991.)

11. **SIAS No. 11 — 1992 Omnibus Statement**
This SIAS has been codified into the following Guidelines:
a. Guidelines 420.01.5 (m).
b. Guidelines 420.01.5 (p) and (q).
c. Guideline 430.01, subsections .3 and .4.
d. Guideline 430.03.1, subsections .a and .b.
e. Guideline 430.04.7, subsections .d and .e.
Additionally, the Introduction to the *Standards* and *General Standard 300 –* Scope of Work have been modified. Also, the Background section of *SIAS No. 11* has been omitted.
(Issued December 1992.)

12. **SIAS No. 12 — Planning the Audit Assignment**
This SIAS has been codified into original Guidelines 410.01, subsections .1-.8b.
Also, the Background section of *SIAS No. 12* has been omitted.
(Issued December 1992.)

13. *SIAS No. 13* — Follow-Up on Reported Audit Findings
This SIAS has been codified into original Guidelines 440.01,
subsections .1-.13e.
Also, the Background section of *SIAS No. 13* has been omitted.
(Issued March 1993.)

14. *SIAS No. 14* — Glossary
This SIAS has been codified into a separate section called
Glossary.
(Issued December 1995.)

15. *SIAS No. 15* — Supervision
This SIAS has been codified into Guidelines 230.01-.06.
Specific Standards 210 and 230 and Guidelines 200.01 and
420.01.5j have been modified. Also, certain redundant material from Guideline 560.02 has been omitted.
(Issued December 1996.)

16. *SIAS No. 16* — Auditing Compliance with Policies, Plans, Procedures, Laws, Regulations, and Contracts
This SIAS has been codified into original Guidelines 320.01,
subsections .1-.8.
Additionally, Specific Standard 320 and Guidelines 300.05,
320.01, and 410.01.2a have been modified.
(Issued April 1997.)

17. *SIAS No. 17* — Assessment of Performance of External Auditors
This SIAS has been codified into Guidelines 550.01, subsections .5-.9.
(Issued April 1997.)

18. *SIAS No. 18* — Use of Outside Service Providers
This SIAS has been codified into Guidelines 220.02, subsections .1-.13.
Additionally, Guidelines 250.01.4, 520.04.5g, and 560.04.3
have been modified.
(Issued December 1997.)

Framework for the *Standards for the Professional Practice of Internal Auditing (Administrative Directive No. 1)*

Purpose

This section establishes the framework for the *Standards for the Professional Practice of Internal Auditing (Standards)* and sets forth the final approval authority required by The Institute of Internal Auditors (IIA) to promulgate the *Standards* and other Standards-related pronouncements (Standards Pronouncements).

Framework

The Framework for the *Standards for the Professional Practice of Internal Auditing* includes the following:

Standards Pronouncements	Final Approval Authority	Description
Statement of Responsibilities of Internal Auditing	IIA Board of Directors	Provides in summary form a general understanding of the responsibilities of internal auditing.
Code of Ethics	IIA Board of Directors	Sets forth standards of conduct for IIA Members and Certified Internal Auditors.
Standards for the Professional Practice of Internal Auditing (the *Standards*)		Describes the criteria by which the operations of an internal auditing department are evaluated and measured.

Standards Pronouncements	Final Approval Authority	Description
– General Standards	IIA Board of Directors	States the five General Standards which should be followed to comply with the *Standards*.
– Specific Standards	Internal Auditing Standards Board (IASB)	States the 25 Specific Standards which should be followed to comply with the General Standards.
– Guidelines	IASB	Describes suitable means of meeting the General and Specific Standards.
Statements on Internal Auditing Standards (SIASs)	IASB	Provides authoritative interpretations of the *Standards*. SIASs are used to add or change existing General Standards, Specific Standards, and Guidelines.
Professional Standards Practice Release (PSPR)	IASB Chairman	Addresses questions resulting from the application of The IIA's Standards Pronouncements. PSPRs are not authoritative positions of the IASB. For authoritative guidance, reference should be made to the *Statement of Responsibilities of Internal Auditing,* the *Code of Ethics,* the *Standards,* and *SIASs.*

Introduction

Internal auditing is an independent appraisal function established within an organization to examine and evaluate its activities as a service to the organization. The objective of internal auditing is to assist members of the organization in the effective discharge of their responsibilities. To this end, internal auditing furnishes them with analyses, appraisals, recommendations, counsel, and information concerning the activities reviewed. The audit objective includes promoting effective control at reasonable cost.

The members of the organization assisted by internal auditing include those in management and the board. Internal auditors owe a responsibility to both, providing them with information about the adequacy and effectiveness of the organization's system of internal control and the quality of performance. The information furnished to each may differ in format and detail, depending upon the requirements and requests of management and the board.

The internal auditing department is an integral part of the organization and functions under the policies established by senior management and the board. The statement of purpose, authority, and responsibility (charter) for the internal auditing department, approved by senior management and accepted by the board, should be consistent with these *Standards for the Professional Practice of Internal Auditing.*

The charter should make clear the purposes of the internal auditing department, specify the unrestricted scope of its work, and declare that auditors are to have no authority or responsibility for the activities they audit.

Throughout the world internal auditing is performed in diverse environments and within organizations which vary in purpose, size, and structure. In addition, the laws and customs within various countries differ from one another. These differences may affect the practice of internal auditing in each environment.

The implementation of these *Standards*, therefore, will be governed by the environment in which the internal auditing department carries out its assigned responsibilities. Compliance with the concepts enunciated by the *Standards* is essential before the responsibilities of internal auditors can be met. As stated in the *Code of Ethics*, Members of The Institute of Internal Auditors and Certified Internal Auditors shall adopt suitable means to comply with the *Standards*.

Independence, as used in the *Standards*, requires clarification. Internal auditors should be independent of the activities they audit. Such independence permits internal auditors to perform their work freely and objectively. Without independence, the desired results of internal auditing cannot be realized.

In establishing the *Standards*, the following matters were considered:
1. Boards of directors are being held accountable for the adequacy and effectiveness of their organizations' systems of internal control and quality of performance.
2. Members of management are relying upon internal auditing as a means of supplying objective analyses, appraisals, recommendations, counsel, and information on the organization's controls and performance.
3. External auditors are using the results of internal audits to complement their own work where the internal auditors have provided suitable evidence of independence and adequate, professional audit work.

In the light of such matters, the purposes of the *Standards* are to:
1. Impart an understanding of the role and responsibilities of internal auditing to all levels of management, boards of directors, public bodies, external auditors, and related professional organizations.
2. Establish the basis for the guidance and measurement of internal auditing performance.
3. Improve the practice of internal auditing.

The *Standards* differentiate among the varied responsibilities of the organization, the internal auditing department, the director of internal auditing, and internal auditors.

The five General Standards are expressed in bold italicized print in uppercase. Following each of these General Standards are Specific Standards expressed in bold italicized print in lowercase. Accompanying the General and Specific Standards are Guidelines describing suitable means of meeting that standard.

The *Standards* encompass:
1. The independence of the internal auditing department from the activities audited and the objectivity of internal auditors.
2. The proficiency of internal auditors and the professional care they should exercise.
3. The scope of internal auditing work.
4. The performance of internal auditing assignments.
5. The management of the internal auditing department.

The *Standards* and the accompanying Guidelines employ terms which have been given meanings in the context of the *Standards*. These terms are included in the Glossary.

Summary of General and Specific *Standards for the Professional Practice of Internal Auditing*

100 **INDEPENDENCE** — *INTERNAL AUDITORS SHOULD BE INDEPENDENT OF THE ACTIVITIES THEY AUDIT.*

    110 **Organizational Status** — *The organizational status of the internal auditing department should be sufficient to permit the accomplishment of its audit responsibilities.*

    120 **Objectivity** —*Internal auditors should be objective in performing audits.*

200 **PROFESSIONAL PROFICIENCY** — *INTERNAL AUDITS SHOULD BE PERFORMED WITH PROFICIENCY AND DUE PROFESSIONAL CARE.*

The Internal Auditing Department

    210 **Staffing** — *The director of internal auditing should ensure that the technical proficiency and educational background of internal auditors are appropriate for the audits to be performed.*

    220 **Knowledge, Skills, and Disciplines** — *The internal auditing department should possess or should obtain the knowledge, skills, and disciplines needed to carry out its audit responsibilities.*

    230 **Supervision** — *The director of internal auditing should ensure that internal audits are properly supervised.*

The Internal Auditor

    240 **Compliance with Standards of Conduct** — *Internal auditors should comply with professional standards of conduct.*

    250 **Knowledge, Skills, and Disciplines** — *Internal auditors should possess the knowledge, skills, and disciplines essential to the performance of internal audits.*

260 Human Relations and Communications — *Internal auditors should be skilled in dealing with people and in communicating effectively.*

270 Continuing Education — *Internal auditors should maintain their technical competence through continuing education.*

280 Due Professional Care — *Internal auditors should exercise due professional care in performing internal audits.*

300 SCOPE OF WORK — *THE SCOPE OF INTERNAL AUDITING SHOULD ENCOMPASS THE EXAMINATION AND EVALUATION OF THE ADEQUACY AND EFFECTIVENESS OF THE ORGANIZATION'S SYSTEM OF INTERNAL CONTROL AND THE QUALITY OF PERFORMANCE IN CARRYING OUT ASSIGNED RESPONSIBILITIES.*

310 Reliability and Integrity of Information — *Internal auditors should review the reliability and integrity of financial and operating information and the means used to identify, measure, classify, and report such information.*

320 Compliance with Policies, Plans, Procedures, Laws, Regulations, and Contracts — *Internal auditors should review the systems established to ensure compliance with those policies, plans, procedures, laws, regulations, and contracts which could have a significant impact on operations and reports, and should determine whether the organization is in compliance.*

330 Safeguarding of Assets — *Internal auditors should review the means of safeguarding assets and, as appropriate, verify the existence of such assets.*

340 Economical and Efficient Use of Resources — *Internal auditors should appraise the economy and efficiency with which resources are employed.*

350 Accomplishment of Established Objectives and Goals for Operations or Programs — *Internal auditors should review operations or programs to ascertain whether results are consistent with es-*

tablished objectives and goals and whether the operations or programs are being carried out as planned.

400 **PERFORMANCE OF AUDIT WORK** — *AUDIT WORK SHOULD INCLUDE PLANNING THE AUDIT, EXAMINING AND EVALUATING INFORMATION, COMMUNICATING RESULTS, AND FOLLOWING UP.*

410 **Planning the Audit** — *Internal auditors should plan each audit.*

420 **Examining and Evaluating Information** — *Internal auditors should collect, analyze, interpret, and document information to support audit results.*

430 **Communicating Results** — *Internal auditors should report the results of their audit work.*

440 **Following Up** — *Internal auditors should follow up to ascertain that appropriate action is taken on reported audit findings.*

500 **MANAGEMENT OF THE INTERNAL AUDITING DEPARTMENT** — *THE DIRECTOR OF INTERNAL AUDITING SHOULD PROPERLY MANAGE THE INTERNAL AUDITING DEPARTMENT.*

510 **Purpose, Authority, and Responsibility** — *The director of internal auditing should have a statement of purpose, authority, and responsibility for the internal auditing department.*

520 **Planning** — *The director of internal auditing should establish plans to carry out the responsibilities of the internal auditing department.*

530 **Policies and Procedures** — *The director of internal auditing should provide written policies and procedures to guide the audit staff.*

540 **Personnel Management and Development** — *The director of internal auditing should establish a program for selecting and developing the human resources of the internal auditing department.*

550 **External Auditors** — *The director of internal auditing should coordinate internal and external audit efforts.*

560   Quality Assurance — *The director of internal auditing should establish and maintain a quality assurance program to evaluate the operations of the internal auditing department.*

100   INDEPENDENCE
INTERNAL AUDITORS SHOULD BE INDEPENDENT
OF THE ACTIVITIES THEY AUDIT.

.01   Internal auditors are independent when they can
carry out their work freely and objectively. Independence permits internal auditors to render the
impartial and unbiased judgments essential to the
proper conduct of audits. It is achieved through
organizational status and objectivity.

110   *Organizational Status*
The organizational status of the internal auditing de-
partment should be sufficient to permit the accomplish-
ment of its audit responsibilities.

.01   Internal auditors should have the support of senior management and of the board so that they
can gain the cooperation of auditees and perform
their work free from interference.

.1   The director of the internal auditing department should be responsible to an individual
in the organization with sufficient authority
to promote independence and to ensure broad
audit coverage, adequate consideration of audit reports, and appropriate action on audit
recommendations.

.2   The director should have direct communication with the board. Regular communication
with the board helps assure independence and
provides a means for the board and the director to keep each other informed on matters of
mutual interest.

a.   Direct communication occurs when the
director regularly attends and participates
in those meetings of the board which relate to its oversight responsibilities for
auditing, financial reporting, organizational governance and control. The
director's attendance at these meetings and
the presentation of written and/or oral reports provides for an exchange of informa-

tion concerning the plans and activities of the internal auditing department. The director of internal auditing should meet privately with the board at least annually.

.3   Independence is enhanced when the board concurs in the appointment or removal of the director of the internal auditing department.

.4   The purpose, authority, and responsibility of the internal auditing department should be defined in a formal written document (charter). The director should seek approval of the charter by senior management as well as acceptance by the board. The charter should (a) establish the department's position within the organization; (b) authorize access to records, personnel, and physical properties relevant to the performance of audits; and (c) define the scope of internal auditing activities.

a.   The director of internal auditing should periodically assess whether the purpose, authority, and responsibility, as defined in the charter, continue to be adequate to enable the internal auditing department to accomplish its objectives. The result of this periodic assessment should be communicated to senior management and the board.

.5   The director of internal auditing should submit annually to senior management for approval and to the board for its information a summary of the department's audit work schedule, staffing plan, and financial budget. The director should also submit all significant interim changes for approval and information. Audit work schedules, staffing plans, and financial budgets should inform senior management and the board of the scope of internal auditing work and of any limitations placed on that scope.

a. The approved audit work schedule, staffing plan, and financial budget, along with all significant interim changes, should contain sufficient information to enable the board to ascertain whether the internal auditing department's objectives and plans support those of the organization and the board. This information should be communicated, preferably in writing.

b. A scope limitation is a restriction placed upon the internal auditing department that precludes the department from accomplishing its objectives and plans. Among other things, a scope limitation may restrict the:

— Scope defined in the charter.
— Department's access to records, personnel, and physical properties relevant to the performance of audits.
— Approved audit work schedule.
— Performance of necessary auditing procedures.
— Approved staffing plan and financial budget.

c. A scope limitation along with its potential effect should be communicated, preferably in writing, to the board.

d. The director of internal auditing should consider whether it is appropriate to inform the board regarding scope limitations which were previously communicated to and accepted by the board. This may be necessary particularly when there have been organization, board, senior management, or other changes.

.6 The director of internal auditing should submit activity reports to senior management and to the board annually or more frequently as necessary. Activity reports should highlight significant audit findings and recommendations and should inform senior management and the board of any significant deviations from approved audit work schedules, staffing plans, and financial budgets, and the reasons for them.

a. Activity reports should be communicated, preferably in writing.

b. Significant audit findings are those conditions which, in the judgment of the director of internal auditing, could adversely affect the organization. Significant audit findings may include conditions dealing with irregularities, illegal acts, errors, inefficiency, waste, ineffectiveness, conflicts of interest, and control weaknesses. After reviewing such findings with senior management, the director of internal auditing should communicate significant audit findings to the board, whether or not they have been satisfactorily resolved.

c. Management's responsibility is to make decisions on the appropriate action to be taken regarding significant audit findings. Senior management may decide to assume the risk of not correcting the reported condition because of cost or other considerations. The board should be informed of senior management's decision on all significant audit findings.

d. The director of internal auditing should consider whether it is appropriate to inform the board regarding previously reported, significant audit findings in those instances when senior management and the board assumed the risk of not correcting the reported condition. This may be necessary, particularly when there have been organization, board, senior management, or other changes.

e. The reasons for significant deviations from approved audit work schedules, staffing plans, and financial budgets that may require explanation include:
— Organization and management changes.
— Economic conditions.
— Legal and regulatory requirements.
— Internal auditing staff changes.
— Management requests.
— Expansion or reduction of audit scope as determined by the director of internal auditing.

120 *Objectivity*
Internal auditors should be objective in performing audits.

.01 Objectivity is an independent mental attitude which internal auditors should maintain in performing audits. Internal auditors are not to subordinate their judgment on audit matters to that of others.

.02 Objectivity requires internal auditors to perform audits in such a manner that they have an honest belief in their work product and that no significant quality compromises are made. Internal auditors are not to be placed in situations in which they feel unable to make objective professional judgments.

.1 Staff assignments should be made so that potential and actual conflicts of interest and bias are avoided. The director should periodically obtain from the internal auditing staff information concerning potential conflicts of interest and bias.

.2 Internal auditors should report to the director any situations in which a conflict of interest or bias is present or may reasonably be inferred. The director should then reassign such auditors.

.3   Staff assignments of internal auditors should be rotated periodically whenever it is practicable to do so.

.4   Internal auditors should not assume operating responsibilities. But if on occasion senior management directs internal auditors to perform nonaudit work, it should be understood that they are not functioning as internal auditors. Moreover, objectivity is presumed to be impaired when internal auditors audit any activity for which they had authority or responsibility. This impairment should be considered when reporting audit results.

.5   Persons transferred to or temporarily engaged by the internal auditing department should not be assigned to audit those activities they previously performed until a reasonable period of time has elapsed. Such assignments are presumed to impair objectivity and should be considered when supervising the audit work and reporting audit results.

.6   The results of internal auditing work should be reviewed before the related audit report is released to provide reasonable assurance that the work was performed objectively.

.03   The internal auditor's objectivity is not adversely affected when the auditor recommends standards of control for systems or reviews procedures before they are implemented. Designing, installing, and operating systems are not audit functions. Also, the drafting of procedures for systems is not an audit function. Performing such activities is presumed to impair audit objectivity.

200   PROFESSIONAL PROFICIENCY
INTERNAL AUDITS SHOULD BE PERFORMED WITH
PROFICIENCY AND DUE PROFESSIONAL CARE.

.01 Professional proficiency is the responsibility of the director of internal auditing and each internal auditor. The director should ensure that persons assigned to each audit collectively possess the necessary knowledge, skills, and disciplines to conduct the audit properly.

The Internal Auditing Department

210   *Staffing*
The director of internal auditing should ensure that the technical proficiency and educational background of internal auditors are appropriate for the audits to be performed.

.01 The director of internal auditing should establish suitable criteria of education and experience for filling internal auditing positions, giving due consideration to scope of work and level of responsibility.

.02 Reasonable assurance should be obtained as to each prospective auditor's qualifications and proficiency.

220   *Knowledge, Skills, and Disciplines*
The internal auditing department should possess or should obtain the knowledge, skills, and disciplines needed to carry out its audit responsibilities.

.01 The internal auditing staff should collectively possess the knowledge and skills essential to the practice of the profession within the organization. These attributes include proficiency in applying internal auditing standards, procedures, and techniques.

.02 The internal auditing department should have employees or use outside service providers who are qualified in disciplines such as accounting, auditing, economics, finance, statistics, information technology, engineering, taxation, law, environmental affairs, and such other areas as needed to meet the department's audit responsibilities. Each member of the department, however, need not be qualified in all disciplines.

.1   An outside service provider is a person or firm, independent of the organization, who has special knowledge, skill, and experience in a particular discipline. Outside service providers include, among others, actuaries, accountants, appraisers, environmental specialists, fraud investigators, lawyers, engineers, geologists, security specialists, statisticians, information technology specialists, the organization's external auditors, and other auditing organizations. An outside service provider may be engaged by the board, senior management, or the director of internal auditing.

.2   Outside service providers may be used by the internal auditing department in connection with, among other things:

   a.   Auditing activities where a specialized skill and knowledge are required such as information technology, statistics, taxes, language translations, or to achieve the objectives in the audit work schedule.

   b.   Valuations of assets such as land and buildings, works of art, precious gems, investments, and complex financial instruments.

   c.   Determination of quantities or physical condition of certain assets such as mineral and petroleum reserves.

   d.   Measuring the work completed and to be completed on contracts in progress.

   e.   Fraud and security investigations.

   f.   Determination of amounts by using specialized methods such as actuarial determinations of employee benefit obligations.

   g.   Interpretation of legal, technical, and regulatory requirements.

h. Evaluating the internal auditing department's quality assurance program in accordance with Section 560 of the *Standards*.

i. Mergers and acquisitions.

.3 When the director of internal auditing intends to use and rely on the work of an outside service provider, the director should assess the competency, independence, and objectivity of the outside service provider as it relates to the particular assignment to be performed. This assessment should also be made when the outside service provider is selected by senior management or the board, and the director intends to use and rely on the outside service provider's work. When the selection is made by others and the assessment determines that the director should not use and rely on the work of an outside service provider, then the results of the assessment should be communicated to senior management or the board, as appropriate.

.4 The director of internal auditing should determine that the outside service provider possesses the necessary knowledge, skills, and ability to perform the assignment. When assessing competency, the director should consider the following:

a. Professional certification, license, or other recognition of the outside service provider's competency in their particular discipline.

b. Membership of the outside service provider in an appropriate professional organization and adherence to that organization's code of ethics.

c. The reputation of the outside service provider. This may include contacting others familiar with the outside service provider's work.

d. The outside service provider's experience in the type of work being considered.

e. The extent of education and training received by the outside service provider in disciplines that pertain to the particular assignment.

f. The outside service provider's knowledge and experience in the industry in which the organization operates.

.5 The director of internal auditing should assess the relationship of the outside service provider to the organization and to the internal auditing department to ensure that independence and objectivity are maintained throughout the assignment. In performing the assessment, the director of internal auditing should determine that there are no financial, organizational, or personal relationships that will prevent the outside service provider from rendering impartial and unbiased judgments and opinions when performing or reporting on the assignment.

.6 In assessing the independence and objectivity of the outside service provider, the director of internal auditing should consider:

a. The financial interest the provider may have in the organization.

b. The personal or professional affiliation the provider may have to the board, senior management, or others within the organization.

c. The relationship the provider may have had with the organization or the activities being reviewed.

d. The extent of other ongoing services the provider may be performing for the organization.

e. Compensation or other incentives that the provider may have.

.7 If the outside service provider is also the organization's external auditor and the nature of the assignment is extended audit services, the director should ascertain that work performed does not impair the external auditor's independence. Extended audit services refers to those services beyond the requirements of auditing standards generally accepted by external auditors. If the organization's external auditors act or appear to act as members of senior management, management, or as employees of the organization, then their independence may be impaired. Additionally, external auditors may provide the organization with other services such as tax and consulting. Independence, however, should be assessed in relation to the full range of services provided to the organization.

.8 The director of internal auditing should obtain sufficient information regarding the scope of the outside service provider's work. This is necessary in order to ascertain that the scope of work is adequate for the purposes of the internal auditing department.

.9 The director of internal auditing should review with the outside service provider:
   a. Objectives and scope of work.
   b. Specific matters expected to be covered in the report to be rendered, if applicable.
   c. Access to relevant records, personnel, and physical properties.
   d. Information regarding assumptions and procedures to be employed.
   e. Ownership and custody of audit working papers, if applicable.
   f. Confidentiality and restrictions on information obtained during the assignment.

It may be preferable to have these and other matters documented in an engagement letter or contract.

.10 Where the outside service provider performs internal auditing activities, the director of internal auditing should specify and ensure that the work complies with the *Standards for the Professional Practice of Internal Auditing*.

.11 In reviewing the work of an outside service provider, the director of internal auditing should evaluate the adequacy of work performed. This evaluation should include sufficiency of information obtained to afford a reasonable basis for the conclusions reached and the resolution of significant exceptions or other unusual matters.

.12 When the director of internal auditing issues an audit report, and an outside service provider was used, the director may, as appropriate, refer to such services provided.

.13 The outside service provider should be informed or, if appropriate, concurrence should be obtained, prior to making such reference in the report.

230   *Supervision*

The director of internal auditing should ensure that internal audits are properly supervised.

.01 The director of internal auditing is responsible for ensuring that appropriate audit supervision is provided. Supervision is a process which begins with planning and continues throughout the examination, evaluation, report, and follow-up phases of the audit assignment.

.02 Supervision includes:

.1 Ensuring that the auditors assigned possess the requisite knowledge and skills.

.2 Providing appropriate instructions during the planning of the audit and approving the audit program.

.3 Seeing that the approved audit program is carried out unless changes are both justified and authorized.

   .4 Determining that audit working papers adequately support the audit findings, conclusions, and reports.

   .5 Ensuring that audit reports are accurate, objective, clear, concise, constructive, and timely.

   .6 Ensuring that audit objectives are met.

   .7 Providing opportunities for developing internal auditors' knowledge and skills.

.03 Appropriate evidence of supervision should be documented and retained.

.04 The extent of supervision required will depend on the proficiency and experience of internal auditors and the complexity of the audit assignment. Appropriately experienced internal auditors may be utilized to review the work of other internal auditors.

.05 All internal auditing assignments, whether performed by or for the internal auditing department, remain the responsibility of its director. The director is responsible for all significant professional judgments made in the planning, examination, evaluation, report, and follow-up phases of the audit assignment. The director should adopt suitable means to ensure that this responsibility is met. Suitable means include policies and procedures designed to:

   .1 Minimize the risk that professional judgments may be made by internal auditors, or others performing work for the internal auditing department, that are inconsistent with the professional judgment of the director such that a significant adverse effect on the audit assignment could result.

   .2 Resolve differences in professional judgment between the director and internal auditing staff members over significant issues relating to the audit assignment. Such means may include: (a) discussion of pertinent facts; (b) further inquiry and/or research; and (c) documentation and disposition of the differing viewpoints in the audit working papers. In instances of a difference in professional judgment over an ethical issue, suitable means may include referral of the issue to those individuals in the organization having responsibility over ethical matters.

.06   Supervision extends to staff training and development, employee performance evaluation, time and expense control, and similar administrative areas.

The Internal Auditor

240   Compliance with Standards of Conduct
Internal auditors should comply with professional standards of conduct.

.01   The *Code of Ethics* of The Institute of Internal Auditors sets forth standards of conduct and provides a basis for enforcement. The *Code* calls for high standards of honesty, objectivity, diligence, and loyalty to which internal auditors should conform.

250   Knowledge, Skills, and Disciplines
Internal auditors should possess the knowledge, skills, and disciplines essential to the performance of internal audits.

.01   Each internal auditor should possess certain knowledge and skills as follows:

.1   Proficiency in applying internal auditing standards, procedures, and techniques is required in performing internal audits. Proficiency means the ability to apply knowledge to situations likely to be encountered and to deal with them without extensive recourse to technical research and assistance.

.2   Proficiency in accounting principles and techniques is required of auditors who work extensively with financial records and reports.

.3   An understanding of management principles is required to recognize and evaluate the materiality and significance of deviations from good business practice. An understanding means the ability to apply broad knowledge to situations likely to be encountered, to recognize significant deviations, and to be able to carry out the research necessary to arrive at reasonable solutions.

.4 An appreciation is required of the fundamentals of such subjects as accounting, economics, commercial law, taxation, finance, quantitative methods, and information technology. An appreciation means the ability to recognize the existence of problems or potential problems and to determine the further research to be undertaken or the assistance to be obtained.

260 Human Relations and Communications
Internal auditors should be skilled in dealing with people and in communicating effectively.

.01 Internal auditors should understand human relations and maintain satisfactory relationships with auditees.

.02 Internal auditors should be skilled in oral and written communications so that they can clearly and effectively convey such matters as audit objectives, evaluations, conclusions, and recommendations.

270 Continuing Education
Internal auditors should maintain their technical competence through continuing education.

.01 Internal auditors are responsible for continuing their education in order to maintain their proficiency. They should keep informed about improvements and current developments in internal auditing standards, procedures, and techniques. Continuing education may be obtained through membership and participation in professional societies; attendance at conferences, seminars, college courses, and in-house training programs; and participation in research projects.

280   *Due Professional Care*
Internal auditors should exercise due professional care
in performing internal audits.

.01   Due professional care calls for the application of the care and skill expected of a reasonably prudent and competent internal auditor in the same or similar circumstances. Professional care should, therefore, be appropriate to the complexities of the audit being performed. In exercising due professional care, internal auditors should be alert to the possibility of intentional wrongdoing, errors and omissions, inefficiency, waste, ineffectiveness, and conflicts of interest. They should also be alert to those conditions and activities where irregularities are most likely to occur. In addition, they should identify inadequate controls and recommend improvements to promote compliance with acceptable procedures and practices.

.1   Fraud encompasses an array of irregularities and illegal acts characterized by intentional deception. It can be perpetrated for the benefit of or to the detriment of the organization and by persons outside as well as inside the organization.

.2   Fraud designed to benefit the organization generally produces such benefit by exploiting an unfair or dishonest advantage that also may deceive an outside party. Perpetrators of such frauds usually benefit indirectly, since personal benefit usually accrues when the organization is aided by the act. Some examples are:

a.   Sale or assignment of fictitious or misrepresented assets.

b.   Improper payments such as illegal political contributions, bribes, kickbacks, and payoffs to government officials, intermediaries of government officials, customers, or suppliers.

    c. Intentional, improper representation or valuation of transactions, assets, liabilities, or income.

    d. Intentional, improper transfer pricing (e.g., valuation of goods exchanged between related organizations). By purposely structuring pricing techniques improperly, management can improve the operating results of an organization involved in the transaction to the detriment of the other organization.

    e. Intentional, improper related-party transactions in which one party receives some benefit not obtainable in an arm's-length transaction.

    f. Intentional failure to record or disclose significant information to improve the financial picture of the organization to outside parties.

    g. Prohibited business activities such as those which violate government statutes, rules, regulations, or contracts.

    h. Tax fraud.

.3 Fraud perpetrated to the detriment of the organization generally is for the direct or indirect benefit of an employee, outside individual, or another organization. Some examples are:

    a. Acceptance of bribes or kickbacks.

    b. Diversion to an employee or outsider of a potentially profitable transaction that would normally generate profits for the organization.

    c. Embezzlement, as typified by the misappropriation of money or property, and falsification of financial records to cover up the act, thus making detection difficult.

    d. Intentional concealment or misrepresentation of events or data.

    e. Claims submitted for services or goods not actually provided to the organization.

.4 Deterrence of fraud consists of those actions taken to discourage the perpetration of fraud and limit the exposure if fraud does occur. The principal mechanism for deterring fraud is control. Primary responsibility for establishing and maintaining control rests with management.

.5 Internal auditors are responsible for assisting in the deterrence of fraud by examining and evaluating the adequacy and the effectiveness of the system of internal control, commensurate with the extent of the potential exposure/risk in the various segments of the organization's operations. In carrying out this responsibility, internal auditors should, for example, determine whether:

a. The organizational environment fosters control consciousness.

b. Realistic organizational goals and objectives are set.

c. Written policies (e.g., code of conduct) exist that describe prohibited activities and the action required whenever violations are discovered.

d. Appropriate authorization policies for transactions are established and maintained.

e. Policies, practices, procedures, reports, and other mechanisms are developed to monitor activities and safeguard assets, particularly in high-risk areas.

f. Communication channels provide management with adequate and reliable information.

g. Recommendations need to be made for the establishment or enhancement of cost-effective controls to help deter fraud.

.02 Due care implies reasonable care and competence, not infallibility or extraordinary performance.

Due care requires the auditor to conduct examinations and verifications to a reasonable extent, but does not require detailed audits of all transactions. Accordingly, internal auditors cannot give absolute assurance that noncompliance or irregularities do not exist. Nevertheless, the possibility of material irregularities or noncompliance should be considered whenever an internal auditor undertakes an internal auditing assignment.

.1 Detection of fraud consists of identifying indicators of fraud sufficient to warrant recommending an investigation. These indicators may arise as a result of controls established by management, tests conducted by auditors, and other sources both within and outside the organization.

.2 In conducting audit assignments, the internal auditor's responsibilities for detecting fraud are to:

a. Have sufficient knowledge of fraud to be able to identify indicators that fraud may have been committed. This knowledge includes the need to know the characteristics of fraud, the techniques used to commit fraud, and the types of frauds associated with the activities audited.

b. Be alert to opportunities, such as control weaknesses, that could allow fraud. If significant control weaknesses are detected, additional tests conducted by internal auditors should include tests directed toward identification of other indicators of fraud. Some examples of indicators are unauthorized transactions, override of controls, unexplained pricing exceptions, and unusually large product losses. Internal auditors should recognize that the presence of more than one indicator at any one time increases the probability that fraud may have occurred.

c. Evaluate the indicators that fraud may
have been committed and decide whether
any further action is necessary or whether
an investigation should be recommended.
d. Notify the appropriate authorities within
the organization if a determination is made
that there are sufficient indicators of the
commission of a fraud to recommend an
investigation.

.3 Internal auditors are not expected to have
knowledge equivalent to that of a person
whose primary responsibility is detecting and
investigating fraud. Also, audit procedures
alone, even when carried out with due professional care, do not guarantee that fraud will
be detected.

.03 When an internal auditor suspects wrongdoing,
the appropriate authorities within the organization should be informed. The internal auditor may
recommend whatever investigation is considered
necessary in the circumstances. Thereafter, the
auditor should follow up to see that the internal
auditing department's responsibilities have been
met.

.1 Investigation of fraud consists of performing
extended procedures necessary to determine
whether fraud, as suggested by the indicators,
has occurred. It includes gathering sufficient
information about the specific details of a discovered fraud. Internal auditors, lawyers, investigators, security personnel, and other specialists from inside or outside the organization are the parties that usually conduct or
participate in fraud investigations.

.2 When conducting fraud investigations, internal auditors should:

a. Assess the probable level and the extent
of complicity in the fraud within the organization. This can be critical to ensur-

ing that the internal auditor avoids providing information to or obtaining misleading information from persons who may be involved.

b. Determine the knowledge, skills, and disciplines needed to effectively carry out the investigation. An assessment of the qualifications and the skills of internal auditors and of the specialists available to participate in the investigation should be performed to ensure that it is conducted by individuals having the appropriate type and level of technical expertise. This should include assurances on such matters as professional certifications, licenses, reputation, and that there is no relationship to those being investigated or to any of the employees or management of the organization.

c. Design procedures to follow in attempting to identify the perpetrators, extent of the fraud, techniques used, and cause of the fraud.

d. Coordinate activities with management personnel, legal counsel, and other specialists as appropriate throughout the course of the investigation.

e. Be cognizant of the rights of alleged perpetrators and personnel within the scope of the investigation and the reputation of the organization itself.

.3 Once a fraud investigation is concluded, internal auditors should assess the facts known in order to:

a. Determine if controls need to be implemented or strengthened to reduce future vulnerability.

b. Design audit tests to help disclose the existence of similar frauds in the future.

       c. Help meet the internal auditor's responsibility to maintain sufficient knowledge of fraud and thereby be able to identify future indicators of fraud.

.4 Reporting of fraud consists of the various oral or written, interim or final communications to management regarding the status and results of fraud investigations.

.5 A preliminary or final report may be desirable at the conclusion of the detection phase. The report should include the internal auditor's conclusion as to whether sufficient information exists to conduct an investigation. It should also summarize findings that serve as the basis for such decision.

.6 Section 430 of the *Standards* provides interpretations applicable to internal audit reports issued as a result of fraud investigations. Additional interpretive guidelines on reporting of fraud are as follows:

       a. When the incidence of significant fraud has been established to a reasonable certainty, senior management and the board should be notified immediately.

       b. The results of a fraud investigation may indicate that fraud has had a previously undiscovered significant adverse effect on the financial position and results of operations of an organization for one or more years on which financial statements have already been issued. Internal auditors should inform senior management and the board of such a discovery.

       c. A written report should be issued at the conclusion of the investigation phase. It should include all findings, conclusions, recommendations, and corrective action taken.

     d. A draft of the proposed report on fraud should be submitted to legal counsel for review. In those cases in which the internal auditor wants to invoke client privilege, consideration should be given to addressing the report to legal counsel.

.04 Exercising due professional care means using reasonable audit skill and judgment in performing the audit. To this end, the internal auditor should consider:

    .1 The extent of audit work needed to achieve audit objectives.

    .2 The relative materiality or significance of matters to which audit procedures are applied.

    .3 The adequacy and effectiveness of internal controls.

    .4 The cost of auditing in relation to potential benefits.

.05 Due professional care includes evaluating established operating standards and determining whether those standards are acceptable and are being met. When such standards are vague, authoritative interpretations should be sought. If internal auditors are required to interpret or select operating standards, they should seek agreement with auditees as to the standards needed to measure operating performance.

300   SCOPE OF WORK
THE SCOPE OF INTERNAL AUDITING SHOULD
ENCOMPASS THE EXAMINATION AND EVALUA-
TION OF THE ADEQUACY AND EFFECTIVENESS OF
THE ORGANIZATION'S SYSTEM OF INTERNAL
CONTROL AND THE QUALITY OF PERFORMANCE
IN CARRYING OUT ASSIGNED RESPONSIBILITIES.

.01   The scope of internal auditing work, as specified
      in this standard, encompasses what audit work
      should be performed. It is recognized, however,
      that senior management and the board provide
      general direction as to the scope of work and the
      activities to be audited.

.02   The purpose of the review for adequacy of the sys-
      tem of internal control is to ascertain whether the
      system established provides reasonable assurance
      that the organization's objectives and goals will
      be met efficiently and economically.

   .1   Objectives are the broadest statements of what
        the organization chooses to accomplish. The
        establishment of objectives precedes the se-
        lection of goals and the design, implementa-
        tion, and maintenance of systems whose pur-
        pose is to meet the organization's objectives
        and goals.

   .2   Goals are specific objectives of specific sys-
        tems and may be otherwise referred to as op-
        erating or program objectives or goals, operat-
        ing standards, performance levels, targets, or
        expected results. Goals should be identified
        for each system. They should be clearly de-
        fined, measurable, attainable, and consistent
        with established broader objectives; and they
        should explicitly recognize the risks associ-
        ated with not achieving those objectives.

   .3   A system (process, operation, function, or ac-
        tivity) is an arrangement, a set, or a collection
        of concepts, parts, activities, and/or people that
        are connected or interrelated to achieve ob-

jectives and goals. (This definition applies to both manual and automated systems.) A system may also be a collection of subsystems operating together for a common objective or goal.

.4 Adequate control is present if management has planned and organized (designed) in a manner which provides reasonable assurance that the organization's objectives and goals will be achieved efficiently and economically. The system design process begins with the establishment of objectives and goals. This is followed by connecting or interrelating concepts, parts, activities, and/or people in such a manner as to operate together to achieve the established objectives and goals. If system design is properly performed, planned activities should be executed as designed and expected results should be attained.

.5 Reasonable assurance is provided when cost-effective actions are taken to restrict deviations to a tolerable level. This implies, for example, that material errors and improper or illegal acts will be prevented or detected and corrected within a timely period by employees in the normal course of performing their assigned duties. The cost-benefit relationship is considered by management during the design of systems. The potential loss associated with any exposure or risk is weighed against the cost to control it.

.6 Efficient performance accomplishes objectives and goals in an accurate and timely fashion with minimal use of resources.

.7 Economical performance accomplishes objectives and goals at a cost commensurate with the risk. The term efficient incorporates the concept of economical performance.

.03 The purpose of the review for effectiveness of the system of internal control is to ascertain whether the system is functioning as intended.

.1 Effective control is present when management directs systems in such a manner as to provide reasonable assurance that the organization's objectives and goals will be achieved.

.2 Directing involves, in addition to accomplishing objectives and planned activities, authorizing and monitoring performance, periodically comparing actual with planned performance, and documenting these activities to provide additional assurance that systems operate as planned.

a. Authorizing includes initiating or granting permission to perform activities or transactions. Authorization implies that the authorizing authority has verified and validated that the activity or transaction conforms with established policies and procedures.

b. Monitoring encompasses supervising, observing, and testing activities and appropriately reporting to responsible individuals. Monitoring provides an ongoing verification of progress toward achievement of objectives and goals.

c. Periodic comparison of actual to planned performance enhances the likelihood that activities occur as planned.

d. Documenting provides evidence of the exercise of authority and responsibility; compliance with policies, procedures, and standards of performance; supervising, observing, and testing activities; and verification of planned performance.

.04 The purpose of the review for quality of performance is to ascertain whether the organization's objectives and goals have been achieved.

.05   The primary objectives of internal control are to ensure:

   .1   The reliability and integrity of information.

   .2   Compliance with policies, plans, procedures, laws, regulations, and contracts.

   .3   The safeguarding of assets.

   .4   The economical and efficient use of resources.

   .5   The accomplishment of established objectives and goals for operations or programs.

.06   A control is any action taken by management to enhance the likelihood that established objectives and goals will be achieved. Management plans, organizes, and directs the performance of sufficient actions to provide reasonable assurance that objectives and goals will be achieved. Thus, control is the result of proper planning, organizing, and directing by management.

   .1   Controls may be preventive (to deter undesirable events from occurring), detective (to detect and correct undesirable events which have occurred), or directive (to cause or encourage a desirable event to occur).

   .2   All variants of the term control (administrative control, internal accounting control, internal control, management control, operational control, output control, preventive control, etc.) can be incorporated within the generic term. These variants differ primarily in terms of the objectives to be achieved. Since these variants are useful in describing specific control applications, participants in the control process should be familiar with the terms as well as their applications. However, the methodology followed by internal auditors in evaluating such controls is consistent for all of the variants.

   .3   The variant internal control came into general use to distinguish controls within an organization from those existing externally to the organization (such as laws). Since internal auditors operate within an organization and, among other responsibilities, evaluate management's response to external stimuli (such as laws), no such distinction between internal and external controls is necessary. Also, from the organization's viewpoint, internal controls are all activities which attempt to ensure the accomplishment of the organization's objectives and goals. Internal control is considered synonymous with control within the organization.

.4 The overall system of control is conceptual in nature. It is the integrated collection of controlled systems used by an organization to achieve its objectives and goals.

.07 Management plans, organizes, and directs in such a fashion as to provide reasonable assurance that established objectives and goals will be achieved.

.1 Planning and organizing involve the establishment of objectives and goals and the use of such tools as organization charts, flowcharts, procedures, records, and reports to establish the flow of data and the responsibilities of individuals for performing activities, establishing information trails, and setting standards of performance.

.2 Directing involves certain activities to provide additional assurance that systems operate as planned. These activities include authorizing and monitoring performance, periodically comparing actual with planned performance, and appropriately documenting these activities.

.3 Management ensures that its objectives and goals remain appropriate and that its systems remain current. Therefore, management periodically reviews its objectives and goals and modifies its systems to accommodate changes in internal and external conditions.

.4   Management establishes and maintains an environment that fosters control.

.08   Internal auditors examine and evaluate the planning, organizing, and directing processes to determine whether reasonable assurance exists that objectives and goals will be achieved. Such evaluations, in the aggregate, provide information to appraise the overall system of internal control.

.1   All systems, processes, operations, functions, and activities within the organization are subject to the internal auditors' evaluations.

.2   Such evaluations should encompass whether reasonable assurance exists that:
   a.   Objectives and goals have been established.
   b.   Authorizing, monitoring, and periodic comparison activities have been planned, performed, and documented as necessary to attain objectives and goals.
   c.   Planned results have been achieved (objectives and goals have been accomplished).

.3   Internal auditors perform evaluations at specific points in time but should be alert to actual or potential changes in conditions which affect the ability to provide assurance from a forward-looking perspective. In those cases, internal auditors should address the risk that performance may deteriorate.

310   *Reliability and Integrity of Information*
Internal auditors should review the reliability and integrity of financial and operating information and the means used to identify, measure, classify, and report such information.

.01   Information systems provide data for decision making, control, and compliance with external requirements. Therefore, internal auditors should examine information systems and, as appropriate, ascertain whether:

.1 Financial and operating records and reports contain accurate, reliable, timely, complete, and useful information.

.2 Controls over record keeping and reporting are adequate and effective.

320 *Compliance with Policies, Plans, Procedures, Laws, Regulations, and Contracts*
Internal auditors should review the systems established to ensure compliance with those policies, plans, procedures, laws, regulations, and contracts which could have a significant impact on operations and reports, and should determine whether the organization is in compliance.

.01 Management is responsible for establishing the systems designed to ensure compliance with such requirements as policies, plans, procedures, applicable laws and regulations, and contracts. Internal auditors are responsible for determining whether the systems are adequate and effective and whether the activities audited are complying with the appropriate requirements.

.1 The term compliance refers to the ability to reasonably ensure conformity and adherence to organization policies, plans, procedures, laws, regulations, and contracts.

.2 The term compliance requirement refers to conditions established by management for the organization. The term also refers to conditions which may be imposed on the organization by law or regulation, or agreed to by contractual arrangement. These conditions affect the manner in which an organization's operations are conducted and objectives are achieved. Compliance requirements include those established, imposed, or agreed to for the purpose of safeguarding organization assets including prevention and/or detection of unauthorized acquisition, use, or disposition of resources.

.3 Management is responsible for having knowledge of compliance requirements of all laws, regulations, and contracts applicable to the organization which are significant to achieving internal control objectives set forth in Section 300.05 of the *Standards*.

.4 Management is responsible for designing and implementing policies, plans, and procedures, including those intended to comply with laws, regulations, and contracts.

    a. The policies, plans, and procedures designed and implemented by management should be sufficient to reasonably ensure prevention and/or detection of noncompliance with applicable laws, regulations, and contracts that are significant to achieving internal control objectives. Significant noncompliance with laws, regulations, or contracts may constitute illegal acts, as described in Section 280 of the *Standards*. Significant noncompliance can also occur with respect to policies, plans, and procedures in which no law or regulation is involved.

    b. Management is responsible for determining whether noncompliance brought to its attention by internal auditors, or by discovery, may violate laws, regulations, or contractual agreements, and/or constitute illegal acts. In addition, management is responsible for initiating such corrective actions necessary to achieve compliance. This may require reporting by management to the board and appropriate legal, funding, and/or regulatory authorities.

.5 In determining audit objectives, internal auditors should make inquiry regarding specific compliance requirements that are significant to internal control objectives. Internal auditors should consider inquiring about significant compliance requirements with:

a. Organization management having financial, operational, and oversight responsibilities.
b. Internal or external legal counsel.
c. Funding or contracting organizations.
d. Governmental or other regulatory authorities.
e. External auditors.

.6 Internal auditors are responsible for establishing objectives that include planning and performing a scope of work which provides a reasonable basis for reporting on the extent of organization compliance with policies, plans, procedures, laws, regulations, and contracts that are significant to internal control objectives.

.7 Internal auditors may perform additional procedures which provide insight with respect to compliance with laws, regulations, and contracts. Such performance may provide insight as to the existence and impact of exposure to significant instances of noncompliance.

.8 Internal auditors should promptly inform senior management and the board of all relevant facts when information gathered from the performance of internal auditing procedures indicates the existence of significant noncompliance or an unreasonable exposure to significant instances of noncompliance.

330   *Safeguarding of Assets*
Internal auditors should review the means of safeguarding assets and, as appropriate, verify the existence of such assets.

.01 Internal auditors should review the means used to safeguard assets from various types of losses such as those resulting from theft, fire, improper or illegal activities, and exposure to elements.

.02 Internal auditors, when verifying the existence of assets, should use appropriate audit procedures.

340 *Economical and Efficient Use of Resources*
Internal auditors should appraise the economy and efficiency with which resources are employed.

.01 Management is responsible for setting operating standards to measure an activity's economical and efficient use of resources. Internal auditors are responsible for determining whether:

.1 Operating standards have been established for measuring economy and efficiency.

.2 Established operating standards are understood and are being met.

.3 Deviations from operating standards are identified, analyzed, and communicated to those responsible for corrective action.

.4 Corrective action has been taken.

.02 Audits related to the economical and efficient use of resources should identify such conditions as:

.1 Underutilized facilities.

.2 Nonproductive work.

.3 Procedures which are not cost justified.

.4 Overstaffing or understaffing.

350 *Accomplishment of Established Objectives and Goals for Operations or Programs*
Internal auditors should review operations or programs to ascertain whether results are consistent with established objectives and goals and whether the operations or programs are being carried out as planned.

.01 Management is responsible for establishing operating or program objectives and goals, developing and implementing control procedures, and accomplishing desired operating or program results. Internal auditors should ascertain whether such objectives and goals conform with those of the organization and whether they are being met.

.1 The term operations refers to the recurring activities of an organization directed toward producing a product or rendering a service.

Such activities may include, but are not limited to, marketing, sales, production, purchasing, human resources, finance and accounting, and governmental assistance. An operation's results may be measured against established objectives and goals which may include budgets, time or production schedules, and/or operating plans.

.2 The term programs refers to special purpose activities of an organization. Such activities include, but are not limited to, the raising of capital, sale of a facility, fund-raising campaigns, new product or service introduction campaigns, capital expenditures, and special purpose government grants. Special purpose activities may be short-term or long-term, spanning several years. When a program is completed, it generally ceases to exist. Program results may be measured against established program objectives and goals.

.3 Management is responsible for establishing criteria to determine if objectives and goals have been accomplished.

.4 Internal auditors should ascertain whether criteria have been established. If so, internal auditors should use such criteria for evaluation if they are considered adequate.

.5 If management has not established criteria, or if the established criteria, in the internal auditors' opinion, are less than adequate, internal auditors should report such conditions to the appropriate levels of management. Additionally, internal auditors may recommend appropriate courses of action depending on the circumstances.

.6 Internal auditors may recommend alternative sources of criteria to management, such as:
    a. Acceptable industry standards.
    b. Standards developed by professions or associations.

      c. Standards in law and government regulations.

.7 If adequate criteria are not established by management, internal auditors may still formulate criteria they believe to be adequate in order to perform an audit, form an opinion, and issue a report on the accomplishment of established objectives and goals.

.8 The internal auditors' evaluation of the accomplishment of established objectives and goals may be carried out with respect to an entire operation or program or only a portion of it. Audit objectives may include determining whether:

      a. The objectives and goals established by management for a proposed, new, or existing operation or program are adequate and have been effectively articulated and communicated.

      b. The operation or program achieves its desired level of interim or final results.

      c. The factors which inhibit satisfactory performance are identified, evaluated, and controlled in an appropriate manner.

      d. Management has considered alternatives for directing an operation or program which may yield more effective and efficient results.

      e. An operation or program complements, duplicates, overlaps, or conflicts with other operations or programs.

      f. Controls for measuring and reporting the accomplishment of objectives and goals are established and are adequate.

      g. An operation or program is in compliance with policies, plans, procedures, laws, and regulations.

.9 Internal auditors should communicate the audit results to the appropriate levels of management. The report should state the criteria established by management and employed by internal auditors and disclose the nonexistence or inadequacy of any needed criteria. If internal auditors formulated criteria by which to measure the accomplishment of objectives and goals, the report should clearly state that internal auditors formulated the criteria and then present the audit results.

.02 Internal auditors can provide assistance to managers who are developing objectives, goals, and systems by determining whether the underlying assumptions are appropriate; whether accurate, current, and relevant information is being used; and whether suitable controls have been incorporated into the operations or programs.

400   PERFORMANCE OF AUDIT WORK

AUDIT WORK SHOULD INCLUDE PLANNING THE AUDIT, EXAMINING AND EVALUATING INFORMATION, COMMUNICATING RESULTS, AND FOLLOWING UP.

.01   The internal auditor is responsible for planning and conducting the audit assignment, subject to supervisory review and approval.

410   *Planning the Audit*

Internal auditors should plan each audit.

.01   Planning should be documented and should include:

     .1   Establishing audit objectives and scope of work.

        a.   Audit objectives are broad statements developed by internal auditors and define intended audit accomplishments. Audit procedures are the means to attain audit objectives. Audit objectives and procedures, taken together, define the scope of the internal auditor's work.

        b.   Audit objectives and procedures should address the risks associated with the activity under audit. The term risk is the probability that an event or action may adversely affect the activity under audit. The guidelines contained in Sections 520.04.1 - .14 of the *Standards* should be used by internal auditors to assess risk for individual audit assignments.

        c.   The purpose of the risk assessment during the planning phase of the audit is to identify significant areas of the auditable activity.

     .2   Obtaining background information about the activities to be audited.

        a.   A review of background information should be performed to determine the impact on the audit. Such items include:

- Objectives and goals.
- Policies, plans, procedures, laws, regulations, and contracts which could have a significant impact on operations and reports.
- Organizational information, e.g., number and names of employees, key employees, job descriptions, and details about recent changes in the organization, including major system changes.
- Budget information, operating results, and financial data of the activity to be audited.
- Prior audit working papers.
- Results of other audits, including the work of external auditors, completed or in process.
- Correspondence files to determine potential significant audit issues.
- Authoritative and technical literature appropriate to the activity.

b. Other requirements of the audit, such as the audit period covered and estimated completion dates, should be determined. The final audit report format should be considered, since proper planning at this stage facilitates writing the final audit report.

.3 Determining the resources necessary to perform the audit.

a. The number and experience level of the internal auditing staff required should be based on an evaluation of the nature and complexity of the audit assignment, time constraints, and available resources.

b. Knowledge, skills, and disciplines of the internal auditing staff should be considered in selecting internal auditors for the audit assignment.

c. Training needs of internal auditors should be considered, since each audit assignment serves as a basis for meeting developmental needs of the internal auditing department.

d. Consideration of the use of external resources in instances where additional knowledge, skills, and disciplines are needed.

.4 Communicating with all who need to know about the audit.

a. Meetings should be held with management responsible for the activity being examined. Topics of discussion may include:
— Planned audit objectives and scope of work.
— The timing of audit work.
— Internal auditors assigned to the audit.
— The process of communicating throughout the audit, including the methods, time frames, and individuals who will be responsible.
— Business conditions and operations of the activity being audited, including recent changes in management or major systems.
— Concerns or any requests of management.
— Matters of particular interest or concern to the internal auditor.
— Description of the internal auditing department's reporting procedures and follow-up process.

b. A summary of matters discussed at meetings and any conclusions reached should be prepared, distributed to individuals, as appropriate, and retained in the audit working papers.

.5   Performing, as appropriate, a survey to become
familiar with the activities, risks, and controls
to identify areas for audit emphasis, and to
invite auditee comments and suggestions.
a.   A survey is a process for gathering information, without detailed verification, on
the activity being examined. The main
purposes are to:
— Understand the activity under review.
— Identify significant areas warranting
special emphasis.
— Obtain information for use in performing the audit.
— Determine whether further auditing is
necessary.
b.   A survey permits an informed approach
to planning and carrying out audit work,
and is an effective tool for applying the
internal auditing department's resources
where they can be used most effectively.
c.   The focus of a survey will vary depending
upon the nature of the audit.
d.   The scope of work and the time requirements of a survey will vary. Contributing
factors include the internal auditor's training and experience, knowledge of the activity being examined, the type of audit
being performed, and whether the survey
is part of a recurring or follow-up assignment. Time requirements will also be
influenced by the size and complexity of
the activity being examined, and by the
geographical dispersion of the activity.
e.   A survey may involve use of the following procedures:
— Discussions with the auditee.
— Interviews with individuals affected by
the activity, e.g., users of the activity's
output.

— On-site observations.
— Review of management reports and studies.
— Analytical auditing procedures.
— Flowcharting.
— Functional "walk-thru" (tests of specific work activities from beginning to end).
— Documenting key control activities.

f. A summary of results should be prepared at the conclusion of the survey. The summary should identify:

— Significant audit issues and reasons for pursuing them in more depth.
— Pertinent information developed during the survey.
— Audit objectives, audit procedures, and special approaches such as computer-assisted audit techniques.
— Potential critical control points, control deficiencies, and/or excess controls.
— Preliminary estimates of time and resource requirements.
— Revised dates for reporting phases and completing the audit.
— When applicable, reasons for not continuing the audit.

.6 Writing the audit program.

a. Audit programs should:

— Document the internal auditor's procedures for collecting, analyzing, interpreting, and documenting information during the audit.
— State the objectives of the audit.
— Set forth the scope and degree of testing required to achieve the audit objectives in each phase of the audit.

— Identify technical aspects, risks, processes, and transactions which should be examined.

— State the nature and extent of testing required.

— Be prepared prior to the commencement of audit work and modified, as appropriate, during the course of the audit.

.7 Determining how, when, and to whom audit results will be communicated.

   a. The director of internal auditing is responsible for determining how, when, and to whom audit results will be communicated. This determination should be documented and communicated to management, to the extent deemed practical, during the planning phase of the audit. Subsequent changes which affect the timing or reporting of audit results should also be communicated to management, if appropriate.

.8 Obtaining approval of the audit work plan.

   a. Audit work plans should be approved in writing by the director of internal auditing or designee prior to the commencement of audit work.

   b. Adjustments to audit work plans should be approved in a timely manner. Initially, approval may be obtained orally, if factors preclude obtaining written approval prior to commencing audit work.

420 *Examining and Evaluating Information*
Internal auditors should collect, analyze, interpret, and document information to support audit results.

.01 The process of examining and evaluating information is as follows:

   .1 Information should be collected on all matters related to the audit objectives and scope of work.

a. Internal auditors use analytical auditing procedures when examining and evaluating information.
b. Analytical auditing procedures are performed by studying and comparing relationships among both financial and nonfinancial information.
c. The application of analytical auditing procedures is based on the premise that, in the absence of known conditions to the contrary, relationships among information may reasonably be expected to exist and continue. Examples of contrary conditions include unusual or nonrecurring transactions or events; accounting, organizational, operational, environmental, and technological changes; inefficiencies; ineffectiveness; errors; irregularities, or illegal acts.
d. Analytical auditing procedures provide internal auditors with an efficient and effective means of making an assessment of information collected in an audit. The assessment results from comparing such information with expectations identified or developed by the internal auditor.
e. Analytical auditing procedures are useful in identifying, among other things:
   — Differences that are not expected.
   — The absence of differences when they are expected.
   — Potential errors.
   — Potential irregularities or illegal acts.
   — Other unusual or nonrecurring transactions or events.
f. Analytical auditing procedures may include:
   — Comparison of current period information with similar information for prior periods.

- Comparison of current period information with budgets or forecasts.
- Study of relationships of financial information with the appropriate nonfinancial information (for example, recorded payroll expense compared to changes in average number of employees).
- Study of relationships among elements of information (for example, fluctuation in recorded interest expense compared to changes in related debt balances).
- Comparison of information with similar information for other organizational units.
- Comparison of information with similar information for the industry in which the organization operates.

g. Analytical auditing procedures may be performed using monetary amounts, physical quantities, ratios, or percentages.

h. Specific analytical auditing procedures include, but are not limited to, ratio, trend, and regression analysis, reasonableness tests, period-to-period comparisons, comparisons with budgets, forecasts, and external economic information.

i. Analytical auditing procedures assist internal auditors in identifying conditions which may require subsequent auditing procedures. Internal auditors should use analytical auditing procedures in planning the audit in accordance with the guidelines contained in Section 410 of the *Standards*.

j. Analytical auditing procedures should also be used during the audit to examine and evaluate information to support audit results. Internal auditors should consider

the following factors in determining the extent to which analytical auditing procedures should be used:
— The significance of the area being examined.
— The adequacy of the system of internal control.
— The availability and reliability of financial and nonfinancial information.
— The precision with which the results of analytical auditing procedures can be predicted.
— The availability and comparability of information regarding the industry in which the organization operates.
— The extent to which other auditing procedures provide support for audit results.

After evaluating the aforementioned factors, internal auditors should consider and use additional auditing procedures, as necessary, to achieve the audit objective.

k. When analytical auditing procedures identify unexpected results or relationships, internal auditors should examine and evaluate such results or relationships.

l. The examination and evaluation of unexpected results or relationships from applying analytical auditing procedures should include inquiries of management and the application of other auditing procedures until internal auditors are satisfied that the results or relationships are sufficiently explained.

m. Unexplained results or relationships from applying analytical auditing procedures may be indicative of a significant condition such as a potential error, irregularity, or illegal act.

n. Results or relationships from applying analytical auditing procedures that are not sufficiently explained should be communicated to the appropriate levels of management. Internal auditors may recommend appropriate courses of action, depending on the circumstances.

.2 Information should be sufficient, competent, relevant, and useful to provide a sound basis for audit findings and recommendations.

  a. Sufficient information is factual, adequate, and convincing so that a prudent, informed person would reach the same conclusions as the auditor.

  b. Competent information is reliable and the best attainable through the use of appropriate audit techniques.

  c. Relevant information supports audit findings and recommendations and is consistent with the objectives for the audit.

  d. Useful information helps the organization meet its goals.

.3 Audit procedures, including the testing and sampling techniques employed, should be selected in advance, where practicable, and expanded or altered if circumstances warrant.

.4 The process of collecting, analyzing, interpreting, and documenting information should be supervised to provide reasonable assurance that the auditor's objectivity is maintained and that audit goals are met.

.5 Working papers that document the audit should be prepared by the auditor and reviewed by management of the internal auditing department. These papers should record the information obtained and the analyses made and should support the bases for the findings and recommendations to be reported.

a. Audit working papers generally serve to:
   — Provide the principal support for the internal audit report.
   — Aid in the planning, performance, and review of audits.
   — Document whether the audit objectives were achieved.
   — Facilitate third-party reviews.
   — Provide a basis for evaluating the internal auditing department's quality assurance program.
   — Provide support in circumstances such as insurance claims, fraud cases, and lawsuits.
   — Aid in the professional development of the internal auditing staff.
   — Demonstrate the internal auditing department's compliance with the *Standards for the Professional Practice of Internal Auditing.*

b. The organization, design, and content of audit working papers will depend on the nature of the audit. Audit working papers should, however, document the following aspects of the audit process:
   — Planning.
   — The examination and evaluation of the adequacy and effectiveness of the system of internal control.
   — The auditing procedures performed, the information obtained, and the conclusions reached.
   — Review.
   — Reporting.
   — Follow-up.

c. Audit working papers should be complete and include support for audit conclusions reached.

    d. Among other things, audit working papers may include:
- Planning documents and audit programs.
- Control questionnaires, flowcharts, checklists, and narratives.
- Notes and memoranda resulting from interviews.
- Organizational data, such as organization charts and job descriptions.
- Copies of important contracts and agreements.
- Information about operating and financial policies.
- Results of control evaluations.
- Letters of confirmation and representation.
- Analysis and tests of transactions, processes, and account balances.
- Results of analytical auditing procedures.
- The audit report and management's responses.
- Audit correspondence if it documents audit conclusions reached.

    e. Audit working papers may be in the form of paper, tapes, disks, diskettes, films, or other media. If audit working papers are in the form of media other than paper, consideration should be given to generating backup copies.

    f. If internal auditors are reporting on financial information, the audit working papers should document whether the accounting records agree or reconcile with such financial information.

    g. Some audit working papers may be categorized as permanent or carry-forward audit files. These files generally contain information of continuing importance.

h. The director of internal auditing should establish policies for the types of audit working-paper files maintained, stationery used, indexing and other related matters. Standardized audit working papers such as questionnaires and audit programs may improve the efficiency of an audit and facilitate the delegation of audit work.

i. The following are typical audit working-paper preparation techniques:
   — Each audit working paper should contain a heading. The heading usually consists of the name of the organization or activity being examined, a title or description of the contents or purpose of the working paper, and the date or period covered by the audit.
   — Each audit working paper should be signed (or initialed) and dated by the internal auditor.
   — Each audit working paper should contain an index or reference number.
   — Audit verification symbols (tick marks) should be explained.
   — Sources of data should be clearly identified.

j. All audit working papers should be reviewed to ensure that they properly support the audit report and that all necessary auditing procedures have been performed. Evidence of supervisory review should be documented in the audit working papers. The director of internal auditing has overall responsibility for review but may designate appropriately experienced members of the internal auditing department to perform the review.

k. Evidence of supervisory review should consist of the reviewer initialing and dating each working paper after it is reviewed.

l. Other review techniques that provide evidence of supervisory review include completing an audit working-paper review checklist and/or preparing a memorandum specifying the nature, extent, and results of the review.

m. Reviewers may make a written record (review notes) of questions arising from the review process. When clearing review notes, care should be taken to ensure that the working papers provide adequate evidence that questions raised during the review have been resolved. Acceptable alternatives with respect to disposition of review notes are as follows:

— Retain the review notes as a record of the questions raised by the reviewer and the steps taken in their resolution.

— Discard the review notes after the questions raised have been resolved and the appropriate audit working papers have been amended to provide the additional information requested.

n. Audit working papers are the property of the organization.

o. Audit working-paper files should generally remain under the control of the internal auditing department and should be accessible only to authorized personnel.

p. Management and other members of the organization may request access to audit working papers. Such access may be necessary to substantiate or explain audit findings or to utilize audit documentation for other business purposes. These requests for access should be subject to the approval of the director of internal auditing.

q. It is common practice for internal and external auditors to grant access to each other's audit working papers. Access to audit working papers by external auditors should be subject to the approval of the director of internal auditing.

r. There are circumstances where requests for access to audit working papers and reports are made by parties outside the organization other than external auditors. Prior to releasing such documentation, the director of internal auditing should obtain the approval of senior management and/or legal counsel, as appropriate.

s. The director of internal auditing should develop retention requirements for audit working papers. These retention requirements should be consistent with the organization's guidelines and any pertinent legal or other requirements.

430 Communicating Results
Internal auditors should report the results of their audit work.

.01 A signed, written report should be issued after the audit examination is completed. Interim reports may be written or oral and may be transmitted formally or informally.

.1 Interim reports may be used to communicate information which requires immediate attention, to communicate a change in audit scope for the activity under review, or to keep management informed of audit progress when audits extend over a long period. The use of interim reports does not diminish or eliminate the need for a final report.

.2 Summary reports highlighting audit results may be appropriate for levels of management above the auditee. They may be issued separately from or in conjunction with the final report.

.3   The term signed means that the authorized internal auditor's name should be manually signed in the report. Alternatively, the signature may appear on a cover letter. The internal auditor authorized to sign the report should be designated by the director of internal auditing.

.4   If audit reports are distributed by electronic means, a signed version of the report should be kept on file in the internal auditing department.

.02   Internal auditors should discuss conclusions and recommendations at appropriate levels of management before issuing final written reports.

.1   Discussion of conclusions and recommendations is usually accomplished during the course of the audit and/or at post-audit meetings (exit interviews). Another technique is the review of draft audit reports by management of the auditee. These discussions and reviews help ensure that there have been no misunderstandings or misinterpretations of fact by providing the opportunity for the auditee to clarify specific items and to express views of the findings, conclusions, and recommendations.

.2   Although the level of participants in the discussions and reviews may vary by organization and by the nature of the report, they will generally include those individuals who are knowledgeable of detailed operations and those who can authorize the implementation of corrective action.

.03   Reports should be objective, clear, concise, constructive, and timely.

.1   Objective reports are factual, unbiased, and free from distortion. Findings, conclusions, and recommendations should be included without prejudice.

      a. If it is determined that a final audit report contains an error, the director of internal auditing should consider the need to issue an amended report which identifies the information being corrected. The amended audit report should be distributed to all individuals who received the audit report being corrected.

      b. An error is defined as an unintentional misstatement or omission of significant information in a final audit report.

.2 Clear reports are easily understood and logical. Clarity can be improved by avoiding unnecessary technical language and providing sufficient supportive information.

.3 Concise reports are to the point and avoid unnecessary detail. They express thoughts completely in the fewest possible words.

.4 Constructive reports are those which, as a result of their content and tone, help the auditee and the organization and lead to improvements where needed.

.5 Timely reports are those which are issued without undue delay and enable prompt effective action.

.04 Reports should present the purpose, scope, and results of the audit; and, where appropriate, reports should contain an expression of the auditor's opinion.

.1 Although the format and content of the audit reports may vary by organization or type of audit, they should contain, at a minimum, the purpose, scope, and results of the audit.

.2 Audit reports may include background information and summaries. Background information may identify the organizational units and activities reviewed and provide relevant explanatory information. They may also include the status of findings, conclusions, and recommendations from prior reports. There may also be an indication of whether the report covers a scheduled audit or the response to a request. Summaries, if included, should be balanced representations of the audit report content.

.3   Purpose statements should describe the audit objectives and may, where necessary, inform the reader why the audit was conducted and what it was expected to achieve.

.4   Scope statements should identify the audited activities and include, where appropriate, supportive information such as time period audited. Related activities not audited should be identified if necessary to delineate the boundaries of the audit. The nature and extent of auditing performed also should be described.

.5   Results may include findings, conclusions (opinions), and recommendations.

.6   Findings are pertinent statements of fact. Those findings which are necessary to support or prevent misunderstanding of the internal auditor's conclusions and recommendations should be included in the final audit report. Less significant information or findings may be communicated orally or through informal correspondence.

.7   Audit findings emerge by a process of comparing what should be with what is. Whether or not there is a difference, the internal auditor has a foundation on which to build the report. When conditions meet the criteria, acknowledgment in the audit report of satisfactory performance may be appropriate. Findings should be based on the following attributes:

a.   Criteria: The standards, measures, or expectations used in making an evaluation and/or verification (what should exist).

b. Condition: The factual evidence which the internal auditor found in the course of the examination (what does exist).

c. Cause: The reason for the difference between the expected and actual conditions (why the difference exists).

d. Effect: The risk or exposure the auditee organization and/or others encounter because the condition is not the same as the criteria (the impact of the difference). In determining the degree of risk or exposure, internal auditors should consider the effect their audit findings may have on the organization's financial statements.

e. Reported findings may also include recommendations, auditee accomplishments, and supportive information if not included elsewhere.

.8 Conclusions (opinions) are the internal auditor's evaluations of the effects of the findings on the activities reviewed. They usually put the findings in perspective based upon their overall implications. Audit conclusions, if included in the audit report, should be clearly identified as such. Conclusions may encompass the entire scope of an audit or specific aspects. They may cover, but are not limited to, whether operating or program objectives and goals conform with those of the organization, whether the organization's objectives and goals are being met, and whether the activity under review is functioning as intended.

.05 Reports may include recommendations for potential improvements and acknowledge satisfactory performance and corrective action.

.1 Recommendations are based on the internal auditor's findings and conclusions. They call for action to correct existing conditions or improve operations. Recommendations may suggest approaches to correcting or enhancing performance as a guide for management in achieving desired results. Recommendations may be general or specific. For example, under some circumstances, it may be desirable to recommend a general course of action and specific suggestions for implementation. In other circumstances, it may be appropriate only to suggest further investigation or study.

.2   Auditee accomplishments, in terms of improvements since the last audit or the establishment of a well-controlled operation, may be included in the audit report. This information may be necessary to fairly represent the existing conditions and to provide a proper perspective and appropriate balance to the audit report.

.06   The auditee's views about audit conclusions or recommendations may be included in the audit report.

.1   As part of the internal auditor's discussions with the auditee, the internal auditor should try to obtain agreement on the results of the audit and on a plan of action to improve operations, as needed. If the internal auditor and auditee disagree about the audit results, the audit report may state both positions and the reasons for the disagreement. The auditee's written comments may be included as an appendix to the audit report. Alternatively, the auditee's views may be presented in the body of the report or in a cover letter.

.07   The director of internal auditing or designee should review and approve the final audit report before issuance and should decide to whom the report will be distributed.

.1   The director of internal auditing or a designee should approve and may sign all final reports.

If specific circumstances warrant, consideration should be given to having the auditor-in-charge, supervisor, or lead auditor sign the report as a representative of the director of internal auditing.

.2 Audit reports should be distributed to those members of the organization who are able to ensure that audit results are given due consideration. This means that the report should go to those who are in a position to take corrective action or ensure that corrective action is taken. The final audit report should be distributed to management of the auditee. Higher-level members in the organization may receive only a summary report. Reports may also be distributed to other interested or affected parties such as external auditors and the board.

.3 Certain information may not be appropriate for disclosure to all report recipients because it is privileged, proprietary, or related to improper or illegal acts. Such information, however, may be disclosed in a separate report. If the conditions being reported involve senior management, report distribution should be to the board of the organization.

440 *Following Up*
Internal auditors should follow up to ascertain that appropriate action is taken on reported audit findings.

.01 Internal auditors should determine that corrective action was taken and is achieving the desired results, or that senior management or the board has assumed the risk of not taking corrective action on reported findings.

.1 Follow-up by internal auditors is defined as a process by which they determine the adequacy, effectiveness, and timeliness of actions taken by management on reported audit findings. Such findings also include relevant findings made by external auditors and others.

.2 Responsibility for follow-up should be defined in the internal auditing department's written charter.

.3 Management is responsible for deciding the appropriate action to be taken in response to reported audit findings. The director of internal auditing is responsible for assessing such management action for the timely resolution of the matters reported as audit findings. In deciding the extent of follow-up, internal auditors should consider procedures of a follow-up nature performed by others in the organization.

.4 As stated in Section 110.01.6(c) of the *Standards*, senior management may decide to assume the risk of not correcting the reported condition because of cost or other considerations. The board should be informed of senior management's decision on all significant audit findings.

.5 The nature, timing, and extent of follow-up should be determined by the director of internal auditing.

.6 Factors which should be considered in determining appropriate follow-up procedures are:
   a. The significance of the reported finding.
   b. The degree of effort and cost needed to correct the reported condition.
   c. The risks that may occur should the corrective action fail.
   d. The complexity of the corrective action.
   e. The time period involved.

.7 Certain reported findings may be so significant as to require immediate action by management. These conditions should be monitored by internal auditors until corrected because of the effect they may have on the organization.

.8 There may also be instances where the director of internal auditing judges that management's oral or written response shows that action already taken is sufficient when weighed against the relative importance of the audit finding. On such occasions, follow-up may be performed as part of the next audit.

.9 Internal auditors should ascertain that actions taken on audit findings remedy the underlying conditions.

.10 The director of internal auditing is responsible for scheduling follow-up activities as part of developing audit work schedules.

.11 Scheduling of follow-up should be based on the risk and exposure involved, as well as the degree of difficulty and the significance of timing in implementing corrective action.

.12 The director of internal auditing should establish procedures to include the following:

    a. A time frame within which management's response to the audit findings is required.

    b. An evaluation of management's response.

    c. A verification of the response (if appropriate).

    d. A follow-up audit (if appropriate).

    e. A reporting procedure that escalates unsatisfactory responses/actions, including the assumption of risk, to the appropriate levels of management.

.13 Techniques used to effectively accomplish follow-up include:

    a. Addressing audit report findings to the appropriate levels of management responsible for taking corrective action.

    b. Receiving and evaluating management responses to audit findings during the audit or within a reasonable time period after the report is issued. Responses are more useful if they include sufficient information for the director of internal auditing to evaluate the adequacy and timeliness of corrective action.

c. Receiving periodic updates from management in order to evaluate the status of management's efforts to correct previously reported conditions.

d. Receiving and evaluating reports from other organizational units assigned responsibility for procedures of a follow-up nature.

e. Reporting to senior management or the board on the status of responses to audit findings.

500   MANAGEMENT OF THE INTERNAL
            AUDITING DEPARTMENT
THE DIRECTOR OF INTERNAL AUDITING SHOULD
PROPERLY MANAGE THE INTERNAL AUDITING
DEPARTMENT.

.01   The director of internal auditing is responsible for
      properly managing the department so that:

    .1   Audit work fulfills the general purposes and
           responsibilities approved by senior manage-
           ment and accepted by the board.

    .2   Resources of the internal auditing department
           are efficiently and effectively employed.

    .3   Audit work conforms to the *Standards for the*
           Professional Practice of Internal Auditing.

510   *Purpose, Authority, and Responsibility*
      The director of internal auditing should have a state-
      ment of purpose, authority, and responsibility for the
      internal auditing department.

.01   The director of internal auditing is responsible for
      seeking the approval of senior management and
      the acceptance by the board of a formal written
      document (charter) for the internal auditing de-
      partment.

520   *Planning*
      The director of internal auditing should establish plans
      to carry out the responsibilities of the internal audit-
      ing department.

.01   These plans should be consistent with the inter-
      nal auditing department's charter and with the
      goals of the organization.

.02   The planning process involves establishing:

    .1   Goals.

    .2   Audit work schedules.

    .3   Staffing plans and financial budgets.

    .4   Activity reports.

.03   The goals of the internal auditing department
      should be capable of being accomplished within
      specified operating plans and budgets and, to the
      extent possible, should be measurable. They

should be accompanied by measurement criteria and targeted dates of accomplishment.

.04 Audit work schedules should include (a) what activities are to be audited; (b) when they will be audited; and (c) the estimated time required, taking into account the scope of the audit work planned and the nature and extent of audit work performed by others. Matters to be considered in establishing audit work schedule priorities should include (a) the date and results of the last audit; (b) financial exposure; (c) potential loss and risk; (d) requests by management; (e) major changes in operations, programs, systems, and controls; (f) opportunities to achieve operating benefits; and (g) changes to and capabilities of the audit staff. The work schedules should be sufficiently flexible to cover unanticipated demands on the internal auditing department.

.1 Risk assessment is a process that is crucial to the development of effective audit work schedules. The risk assessment process includes identification of auditable activities, identification of relevant risk factors, and an assessment of their relative significance.

.2 The term risk is the probability that an event or action may adversely affect the organization.

.3 The effects of risk can involve:

   a. An erroneous decision from using incorrect, untimely, incomplete, or otherwise unreliable information.

   b. Erroneous record keeping, inappropriate accounting, fraudulent financial reporting, financial loss and exposure.

   c. Failure to adequately safeguard assets.

   d. Customer dissatisfaction, negative publicity, and damage to the organization's reputation.

  e. Failure to adhere to organizational policies, plans, and procedures, or not complying with relevant laws and regulations.

  f. Acquiring resources uneconomically or using them inefficiently or ineffectively.

  g. Failure to accomplish established objectives and goals for operations or programs.

.4 The first phase of the risk assessment process is to identify and catalog the auditable activities.

.5 Auditable activities consist of those subjects, units, or systems which are capable of being defined and evaluated. Auditable activities may include:

  a. Policies, procedures, and practices.

  b. Cost centers, profit centers, and investment centers.

  c. General ledger account balances.

  d. Information systems (manual and computerized).

  e. Major contracts and programs.

  f. Organizational units such as product or service lines.

  g. Functions such as information technology, purchasing, marketing, production, finance, accounting, and human resources.

  h. Transaction systems for activities such as sales, collection, purchasing, disbursement, inventory and cost accounting, production, treasury, payroll, and capital assets.

  i. Financial statements.

  j. Laws and regulations.

.6 Risk factors are the criteria used to identify the relative significance of, and likelihood that, conditions and/or events may occur that could adversely affect the organization.

.7   The number of risk factors utilized should be limited, but sufficient to provide the director of internal auditing with confidence that the risk assessment is comprehensive.

.8   Risk factors may include:
a.   Ethical climate and pressure on management to meet objectives.
b.   Competence, adequacy, and integrity of personnel.
c.   Asset size, liquidity, or transaction volume.
d.   Financial and economic conditions.
e.   Competitive conditions.
f.   Complexity or volatility of activities.
g.   Impact of customers, suppliers, and government regulations.
h.   Degree of computerized information systems.
i.   Geographical dispersion of operations.
j.   Adequacy and effectiveness of the system of internal control.
k.   Organizational, operational, technological, or economic changes.
l.   Management judgments and accounting estimates.
m.   Acceptance of audit findings and corrective action taken.
n.   Date and results of previous audits.

.9   The director of internal auditing may decide to weigh the risk factors to signify their relative significance. The weighing of risk factors reflects the director's judgment about the relative impact a factor may have on selecting an activity for audit.

.10   Risk assessment is a systematic process for assessing and integrating professional judgments about probable adverse conditions and/or events. The risk assessment process should provide a means of organizing and integrating professional judgments for development of the audit work schedule. The director of internal auditing should generally assign higher audit priorities to activities with higher risks.

.11 The director should incorporate information from a variety of sources into the risk assessment process. Such sources include, but are not limited to: discussions with the board and various members of management; discussions among management and staff of the internal auditing department; discussions with external auditors; consideration of applicable laws and regulations; analyses of financial and operating data; review of prior audits; and industry or economic trends.

.12 The risk assessment process should lead the director of internal auditing to establish audit work schedule priorities. The director may adjust the planned audit work schedule after considering other information such as coordination with external auditors and requests by management and the board.

.13 There should be a periodic assessment of the effect of any major changes in the catalog of auditable activities or related risk factors which have occurred since the audit work schedule was prepared. Such an assessment will assist the director of internal auditing in making appropriate adjustments to audit priorities and the work schedule.

.14 The risk assessment process should be conducted annually. However, because conditions change, audit priorities determined through the risk assessment process may be reviewed and updated throughout the year.

.05 Staffing plans and financial budgets, including the number of auditors and the knowledge, skills, and disciplines required to perform their work, should be determined from audit work schedules, admin-

istrative activities, education and training requirements, and audit research and development efforts.

.06   Activity reports should be submitted periodically
to senior management and to the board. These
reports should compare (a) performance with the
department's goals and audit work schedules and
(b) expenditures with financial budgets. They
should explain the reason for major variances and
indicate any action taken or needed.

530   Policies and Procedures
The director of internal auditing should provide writ-
ten policies and procedures to guide the audit staff.

.01   The form and content of written policies and procedures should be appropriate to the size and structure of the internal auditing department and the
complexity of its work. Formal administrative and
technical audit manuals may not be needed by all
internal auditing departments. A small internal
auditing department may be managed informally.
Its audit staff may be directed and controlled
through daily, close supervision and written
memoranda. In a large internal auditing department, more formal and comprehensive policies
and procedures are essential to guide the audit staff
in the consistent compliance with the
department's standards of performance.

540   Personnel Management and Development
The director of internal auditing should establish a
program for selecting and developing the human re-
sources of the internal auditing department.

.01   The program should provide for:

.1   Developing written job descriptions for each
level of the audit staff.

.2   Selecting qualified and competent individuals.

.3   Training and providing continuing educational
opportunities for each internal auditor.

.4   Appraising each internal auditor's performance at least annually.

.5   Providing counsel to internal auditors on their
performance and professional development.

550 *External Auditors*
The director of internal auditing should coordinate internal and external audit efforts.

.01 Internal and external auditing work should be coordinated to ensure adequate audit coverage and to minimize duplicate efforts.

.1 The scope of internal auditing work encompasses both financial and operational objectives and activities. The scope of internal auditing work is covered by Section 300 of the *Standards*. On the other hand, the external auditors' ordinary examination is designed to obtain sufficient evidential matter to support an opinion on the overall fairness of the annual financial statements. The scope of the work of external auditors is determined by their professional standards, and they are responsible for judging the adequacy of procedures performed and evidence obtained for purposes of expressing their opinion on the annual financial statements.

.2 Oversight of the work of external auditors, including coordination with the internal auditing department, is generally the responsibility of the board. Actual coordination should be the responsibility of the director of internal auditing. The director of internal auditing will require the support of the board to achieve effective coordination of audit work.

.3 In coordinating the work of internal auditors with the work of external auditors, the director of internal auditing should ensure that work to be performed by internal auditors in fulfillment of Section 300 of the *Standards* does not duplicate the work of external auditors which can be relied on for purposes of internal auditing coverage. To the extent that professional and organizational reporting responsibilities allow, internal auditors should conduct examinations in a manner that allows for maximum audit coordination and efficiency.

.4   The director of internal auditing may agree to perform work for external auditors in connection with their annual audit of the financial statements. Work performed by internal auditors to assist external auditors in fulfilling their responsibility is subject to all relevant provisions of the *Standards for the Professional Practice of Internal Auditing.*

.5   The director of internal auditing should make regular evaluations of the coordination between internal and external auditors. Such evaluations may also include assessments of the overall efficiency and effectiveness of internal and external auditing activities, including aggregate audit cost.

.6   In exercising its oversight role, the board may request the director of internal auditing to assess the performance of external auditors. Such assessments should ordinarily be made in the context of the director of internal auditing's role of coordinating internal and external auditing activities, and should extend to other performance matters only at the specific request of senior management or the board.

.7   Assessments of the performance of external auditors should be based on sufficient information to support the conclusions reached. Assessments of the external auditors' performance with respect to the coordination of internal and external auditing activities should reflect the criteria described in Section 550.02 of the *Standards.*

.8   Assessments of the performance of external auditors extending to matters beyond coordination with the internal auditors may address such additional factors as:

       a. Professional knowledge and experience.
       b. Knowledge of the organization's industry.
       c. Independence.
       d. Availability of specialized services.
       e. Anticipation of and responsiveness to the needs of the organization.
       f. Reasonable continuity of key engagement personnel.
       g. Maintenance of appropriate working relationships.
       h. Achievement of contract commitments.
       i. Delivery of overall value to the organization.

.9 The director of internal auditing should communicate the results of evaluations of coordination between internal and external auditors to senior management and the board along with, as appropriate, any relevant comments about the performance of external auditors.

.10 External auditors may be required by their professional standards to ensure that certain matters are communicated to the board. The director of internal auditing should communicate with external auditors regarding these matters so as to have an understanding of the issues. These matters may include:

       a. Significant control weaknesses.
       b. Errors and irregularities.
       c. Illegal acts.
       d. Management judgments and accounting estimates.
       e. Significant audit adjustments.
       f. Disagreements with management.
       g. Difficulties encountered in performing the audit.

.02 Coordination of audit efforts involves:

.1 Periodic meetings to discuss matters of mutual interest.

    a. Planned audit activities of internal and external auditors should be discussed to assure that audit coverage is coordinated and duplicate efforts are minimized. Sufficient meetings should be scheduled during the audit process to assure coordination of audit work and efficient and timely completion of audit activities, and to determine whether findings from work performed to date require that the scope of planned work be adjusted.

.2 Access to each other's audit programs and working papers.

    a. Access to the external auditors' programs and working papers may be important in order for internal auditors to be satisfied as to the propriety for internal audit purposes of relying on the external auditors' work. Such access carries with it the responsibility for internal auditors to respect the confidentiality of those programs and working papers. Similarly, access to the internal auditors' programs and working papers should be given to external auditors in order for external auditors to be satisfied as to the propriety, for external audit purposes, of relying on the internal auditors' work.

.3 Exchange of audit reports and management letters.

    a. Internal audit reports, management's responses to those reports, and subsequent internal auditing department follow-up reviews should be made available to external auditors. These reports assist external auditors in determining and adjusting the scope of work.

    b. Internal auditors need access to the external auditors' management letters. Matters discussed in management letters assist internal auditors in planning the areas to emphasize in future internal audit work. After review of management letters and initiation of any needed corrective action by appropriate members of management and the board, the director of internal auditing should ensure that appropriate follow-up and corrective action have been taken.

.4   Common understanding of audit techniques, methods, and terminology.

a.   The director of internal auditing should understand the scope of work planned by external auditors and should be satisfied that the external auditors' planned work, in conjunction with the internal auditors' planned work, satisfies the requirements of Section 300 of the *Standards*. Such satisfaction requires an understanding of the level of materiality used by external auditors for planning and the nature and extent of the external auditors' planned procedures.

b.   The director of internal auditing should ensure that the external auditors' techniques, methods, and terminology are sufficiently understood by internal auditors to enable the director of internal auditing to (a) coordinate internal and external auditing work; (b) evaluate, for purposes of reliance, the external auditors' work; and (c) ensure that internal auditors who are to perform work to fulfill the external auditors' objectives can communicate effectively with external auditors.

c.   The director of internal auditing should provide sufficient information to enable external auditors to understand the internal auditors' techniques, methods, and terminology to facilitate reliance by external auditors on work performed using such techniques, methods, and terminology.

   d. It may be more efficient for internal and external auditors to use similar techniques, methods, and terminology to effectively coordinate their work and to rely on the work of one another.

560   *Quality Assurance*
The director of internal auditing should establish and maintain a quality assurance program to evaluate the operations of the internal auditing department.

.01   The purpose of this program is to provide reasonable assurance that internal auditing work conforms with the *Standards for the Professional Practice of Internal Auditing,* the internal auditing department's charter, and other applicable standards. A quality assurance program should include the following elements:
- Supervision.
- Internal reviews.
- External reviews.

.1 The reasonable assurance mentioned in this guideline serves the needs of several constituencies in addition to that of the director of internal auditing. These may include senior management, external auditors, the board, and regulatory agencies, each of whom may have reasons to rely upon the performance of the internal auditing department.

.2 Conformity with applicable standards is more than simply complying with established policies and procedures. It includes performance of the internal auditing department at a high level of efficiency and effectiveness. Quality assurance is essential to achieving such performance, as well as to maintaining the internal auditing department's credibility with those it serves.

.3   A key criterion against which an internal auditing department should be measured is its charter. Consideration of the department's charter should also include an assessment of the charter in terms of the elements specified in Section 110 of the *Standards*.

.4   The following are examples of other applicable standards and potential measurement criteria that should be considered in evaluating the performance of the internal auditing department:

a.   The *Code of Ethics*.

b.   The internal auditing department's objectives, policies, and procedures.

c.   The organization's policies and procedures that apply to the internal auditing department.

d.   Laws, regulations, and government or industry standards which specify auditing and reporting requirements.

e.   Methods for identifying auditable activities, assessing risk, and determining frequency and scope of audits.

f.   Audit planning documents, particularly those submitted to senior management and the board.

g.   The plan of organization, statements of job requirements, position descriptions, and professional development plans of the internal auditing department.

.02   Supervision of the work of internal auditors should be carried out to assure conformance with internal auditing standards, departmental policies, and audit programs.

.1   Adequate supervision is the most fundamental element of a quality assurance program. As such, it provides a foundation upon which internal and external reviews can subsequently be built.

.2   The nature and responsibility for supervision are set forth in Section 230 of the *Standards*, and related guidelines.

.03   Internal reviews should be performed periodically by members of the internal auditing staff to appraise the quality of the audit work performed. These reviews should be performed in the same manner as any other internal audit.

.1   Formal internal reviews are periodic self-assessments of the internal auditing department. These reviews generally are performed by a team or an individual selected by the director of internal auditing. Larger departments may have a person designated as manager of quality assurance or with a similar title and responsibilities.

.2   Internal quality assurance reviews primarily serve the needs of the director of internal auditing, but can also provide senior management and the board with an assessment of the internal auditing department. These reviews should be structured so as to indicate the degree of compliance with the *Standards for the Professional Practice of Internal Auditing*, level of audit effectiveness, and extent of compliance with the organization and departmental policies and standards. The review should also provide recommendations for improvement.

.3   An internal review program, particularly in smaller internal auditing departments, will require adaptations that take into consideration the structure of the department and degree of involvement of the director in individual audits.

.4   When formal internal reviews are not appropriate to the internal auditing department's needs, or to supplement such reviews, the following methods can provide elements of internal review coverage:

a. Reviews by the director of internal auditing, audit managers, or supervisors of a sample of audits (and areas of audit administration) where the work was performed under the direction of other managers or supervisors. As an ongoing process this can provide training, exchange of ideas, and greater uniformity, as well as assurance to the director of internal auditing.

b. Feedback from auditees (in addition to that from personal contact) through the use of questionnaires or surveys, either routinely after each audit or periodically for selected audits. This process will elicit management's perception of the internal auditing department and may also result in suggestions to make it more effective and responsive to management's needs.

.5 The director of internal auditing should initiate and monitor the internal review process. In selecting and instructing the team for an internal review, the director of internal auditing should ensure that the team is qualified and as independent as practicable.

.6 The director should receive a written report of the results of each internal review and ensure that appropriate action is taken. Although the purpose of internal reviews is to assess the effectiveness of the internal auditing department for internal purposes, it may be appropriate for the director to share the results with persons outside the department, such as senior management, the board, and external auditors. Internal reviews can also be useful as part of the self-assessment process in preparation for an external review.

.04   External reviews of the internal auditing department should be performed to appraise the quality of the department's operations. These reviews should be performed by qualified persons who are independent of the organization and who do not have either a real or an apparent conflict of interest. Such reviews should be conducted at least once every three years. On completion of the review, a formal, written report should be issued. The report should express an opinion as to the department's compliance with the *Standards for the Professional Practice of Internal Auditing* and, as appropriate, should include recommendations for improvement.

.1   External reviews can have considerable value to the director and other members of the internal auditing department. Another important purpose of external reviews is to provide independent assurance of quality to senior management, the board, and others such as external auditors who rely on the work of the internal auditing department.

.2   The director of internal auditing should discuss with senior management and the board the nature of an external review in the context of the overall quality assurance program and should involve them in the selection of an external reviewer.

.3   External reviews should be performed by qualified individuals who are independent of the organization and who do not have either a real or an apparent conflict of interest. Qualified individuals are persons with the technical proficiency and educational background appropriate for the audit activities to be reviewed and could include internal auditors from outside the organization or outside service providers. Independent of the organization means not a part of, or under the control of, the organization to which the internal auditing department belongs. In the selection of an external reviewer, consideration should be given to a possible real or apparent conflict of interest which the reviewer may have due to present or past relationships with the organization or its internal auditing department.

.4 Organizations of external auditors in various countries have specified certain limited review procedures that they should consider in evaluating and using the work of the internal auditing department. These relate primarily to quality of work and degree of independence from auditees. These limited review procedures by external auditors usually relate only to their audit of an organization's financial statements and generally would not constitute an external review.

.5 Upon completion of an external review, the review team should issue a formal report containing an opinion as to the department's compliance with the *Standards*. The report should also address compliance with the department's charter and other applicable standards and include appropriate recommendations for improvement. The report should be addressed to the person or organization who requested the review. The director of internal auditing should prepare a written action plan in response to the significant comments and recommendations contained in the report of external review. Appropriate follow-up is also the director's responsibility.

.6 External reviews should be conducted at least once every three years. However, there may be circumstances that justify a different interval. These circumstances include: (a) significant review and monitoring by the board; (b) in-depth reviews by external auditors or others; and (c) the relative stability of the internal auditing department's charter, organization, staff, and catalog of auditable activities. The nature, scope, degree of independence, and overall results of the internal review program should also be considered in determining the external review interval.

.7   External review is an important element of the program for achieving quality assurance. However, if resources are limited, or for other reasons previously noted, the internal auditing department may be currently unable to obtain an external review. In these circumstances, more emphasis should be placed on supervision, periodic internal reviews, and other quality assurance methods that are available to the department. It is the responsibility of the director of internal auditing to annually assess the conditions which restrict an external review. Another interim method is the use of qualified internal groups to conduct a review (e.g., former audit managers in the employ of the organization, other audit directors in a decentralized audit organization, or internal management advisory personnel). However, such a review should not be expected to achieve all of the objectives of an external review.

Glossary

The *Standards* and the accompanying Guidelines employ terms which have been given the following meanings in the context of the *Standards*:

Activity Reports of the internal auditing department highlight significant audit findings and recommendations and inform senior management and the board of any significant deviations from approved audit work schedules, staffing plans, and financial budgets, and the reasons for them. (110.01.6)

Adequate Control is present if management has planned and organized (designed) in a manner which provides reasonable assurance that the organization's objectives and goals will be achieved efficiently and economically. (300.02.4)

Analytical Auditing Procedures are performed by studying and comparing relationships among both financial and nonfinancial information. The application of analytical auditing procedures is based on the premise that, in the absence of known conditions to the contrary, relationships among information may reasonably be expected to exist and continue. Examples of contrary conditions include unusual or nonrecurring transactions or events; accounting, organizational, operational, environmental, and technological changes; inefficiencies; ineffectiveness; errors; irregularities, or illegal acts. (420.01.1 b and c)

Appreciation means the ability to recognize the existence of problems or potential problems and to determine the further research to be undertaken or the assistance to be obtained. (250.01.4)

Audit Objectives are broad statements developed by internal auditors and define intended audit accomplishments. (410.01.1a)

Audit Procedures are the tasks the internal auditor undertakes for collecting, analyzing, interpreting, and documenting information during an audit. Audit procedures are the means to attain audit objectives. (410.01.1a)

Audit Program is a document which lists the audit procedures to be followed during an audit. The audit program also states the objectives of the audit. (410.01.6a)

Audit Report is a signed, written document which presents the purpose, scope, and results of the audit. Results of the audit may include findings, conclusions (opinions), and recommendations. (430.01, 430.04 and 430.04.5)

Audit Scope refers to the activities covered by an internal audit. Audit scope includes, where appropriate:

- Audit objectives.
- Nature and extent of auditing procedures performed.
- Time period audited.
- Related activities not audited in order to delineate the boundaries of the audit. (430.04.4)

Audit Work Schedules include (a) what activities are to be audited; (b) when they will be audited; and (c) the estimated time required, taking into account the scope of the audit work planned and the nature and extent of audit work performed by others. (520.04)

Audit Working Papers record the information obtained, the analyses made, and conclusions reached during an audit. Audit working papers support the bases for the findings and recommendations to be reported. (420.01.5 and 420.01.5c)

Auditable Activities consist of those subjects, units, or systems which are capable of being defined and evaluated. Auditable activities may include:

- Policies, procedures, and practices.
- Cost centers, profit centers, and investment centers.

- General ledger account balances.
- Information systems (manual and computerized).
- Major contracts and programs.
- Organizational units such as product or service lines.
- Functions such as information technology, purchasing, marketing, production, finance, accounting, and human resources.
- Transaction systems for activities such as sales, collection, purchasing, disbursement, inventory and cost accounting, production, treasury, payroll, and capital assets.
- Financial statements.
- Laws and regulations. (520.04.5)

Auditee includes any individual, unit, or activity of the organization that is audited.

Authorization implies that the authorizing authority has verified and validated that the activity or transaction conforms with established policies and procedures. (300.03.2a)

Authorizing includes initiating or granting permission to perform activities or transactions. (300.03.2a)

Board includes boards of directors, audit committees of such boards, heads of agencies or legislative bodies to whom internal auditors report, boards of governors or trustees of nonprofit organizations, and any other designated governing bodies of organizations.

Cause is the reason for the difference between the expected and actual conditions (why the difference exists). (430.04.7c)

Charter of the internal auditing department is a formal written document which defines the department's purpose, authority, and responsibility. The charter should (a) establish the department's position within the organization; (b) authorize access to records, personnel, and physical properties relevant to the performance of audits; and (c) define the scope of internal auditing activities. (110.01.4)

Code of Ethics of The Institute of Internal Auditors (IIA) sets
forth standards of conduct for Members of The IIA and Certified Internal Auditors to effectively discharge their responsibilities. The *Code of Ethics* calls for high standards of
honesty, objectivity, diligence, and loyalty. (240.01)

Compliance refers to the ability to reasonably ensure conformity and adherence to organization policies, plans, procedures, laws, regulations, and contracts. (320.01.1)

Compliance Requirement refers to conditions established by
management for the organization. The term also refers to
conditions which may be imposed on the organization by
law or regulation, or agreed to by contractual agreement.
These conditions affect the manner in which an
organization's operations are conducted and objectives are
achieved. Compliance requirements include those established, imposed, or agreed to for the purpose of safeguarding
organization assets including prevention and/or detection
of unauthorized acquisition, use, or disposition of resources.
(320.01.2)

Conclusions (Opinions) are the internal auditor's evaluations
of the effects of the findings on the activities reviewed.
Conclusions usually put the findings in perspective based
upon their overall implications. (430.04.8)

Condition is the factual evidence which the internal auditor
found in the course of the examination (what does exist).
(430.04.7b)

Conflicts of Interest refers to any relationship which is or ap-
pears to be not in the best interest of the organization. A
conflict of interest would prejudice an individual's ability
to carry out their duties and responsibilities objectively.
(280.01)

Control is any action taken by management to enhance the
likelihood that established objectives and goals will be

achieved. Management plans, organizes, and directs the performance of sufficient actions to provide reasonable assurance that objectives and goals will be achieved. Thus, control is the result of proper planning, organizing, and directing by management. (300.06)

Control Environment refers to the attitude and actions of the board and management regarding the significance of control within the organization. The control environment provides the discipline and structure for the achievement of the primary objectives of the system of internal control.

The control environment includes the following elements:

- Integrity and ethical values.
- Management's philosophy and operating style.
- Organizational structure.
- Assignment of authority and responsibility.
- Human resource policies and practices.
- Competence of personnel. (300.07.4)

Cost-Benefit Relationship means that the potential loss associated with any exposure or risk is weighed against the cost to control it. (300.02.5)

Criteria are the standards, measures, or expectations used in making an evaluation and/or verification (what should exist). (430.04.7a)

Detective Controls are actions taken to detect and correct undesirable events which have occurred. (300.06.1)

Directing involves, in addition to accomplishing objectives and planned activities, authorizing and monitoring performance, periodically comparing actual with planned performance, and documenting these activities to provide additional assurance that systems operate as planned. (300.03.2)

Directive Controls are actions taken to cause or encourage a desirable event to occur. (300.06.1)

Director of Internal Auditing and **Director** identify the top position in an internal auditing department. The term also includes such titles as General Auditor, Chief Internal Auditor, Chief Audit Executive, and Inspector General.

Due Professional Care calls for the application of the care and skill expected of a reasonably prudent and competent internal auditor in the same or similar circumstances. Due professional care is exercised when internal audits are performed in accordance with the *Standards for the Professional Practice of Internal Auditing*. The exercise of due professional care requires that:

- Internal auditors be independent of the activities they audit.
- Internal audits be performed by those persons who collectively possess the necessary knowledge, skills, and disciplines to conduct the audit properly.
- Audit work be planned and supervised.
- Audit reports be objective, clear, concise, constructive, and timely.
- Internal auditors follow up on reported audit findings to ascertain that appropriate action was taken. (280.01)

Economical Performance accomplishes objectives and goals at a cost commensurate with the risk. (300.02.7)

Effect is the risk or exposure the auditee organization and/or others encounter because the condition is not the same as the criteria (the impact of the difference). (430.04.7d)

Effective Control is present when management directs systems in such a manner as to provide reasonable assurance that the organization's objectives and goals will be achieved. (300.03.1)

Efficient Performance accomplishes objectives and goals in an accurate and timely fashion with minimal use of resources. (300.02.6)

Error as it relates to internal audit reports is an unintentional misstatement or omission of significant information in a final audit report. (430.03.1b)

External Auditors refers to those audit professionals who perform independent annual audits of an organization's financial statements.

External Reviews of the internal auditing department are performed to appraise the quality of the department's operations. External reviews should be performed by qualified persons who are independent of the organization and who do not have either a real or apparent conflict of interest. (560.04)

Findings are pertinent statements of fact. Audit findings emerge by a process of comparing what should be with what is. (430.04.6 and .7)

Flowchart is a representation, primarily through the use of symbols, of the sequence of activities in a system (process, operation, function, or activity). (420.01.5d)

Follow-up by internal auditors is defined as a process by which they determine the adequacy, effectiveness, and timeliness of actions taken by management on reported audit findings. Such findings also include relevant findings made by external auditors and others. (440.01.1)

Formal Internal Reviews are periodic self-assessments of the internal auditing department to appraise the quality of the audit work performed. These reviews generally are performed by a team or an individual selected by the director of internal auditing. (560.03.1)

Fraud encompasses an array of irregularities and illegal acts characterized by intentional deception. (280.01.1)

Goals are specific objectives of specific systems and may be otherwise referred to as operating or program objectives or goals, operating standards, performance levels, targets, or expected results. (300.02.2)

Guidelines are suitable means of meeting the General and Specific *Standards for the Professional Practice of Internal Auditing.* (Introduction)

Illegal Acts refers to violations of laws and governmental regulations. (280.01.1)

Independence allows internal auditors to carry out their work freely and objectively. This concept requires that internal auditors be independent of the activities they audit. Independence is achieved through organizational status and objectivity. (100.01)

Information is data the internal auditor obtains during an audit to provide a sound basis for audit findings and recommendations. Information should be sufficient, competent, relevant, and useful. (420.01.2)

Internal Auditing is an independent appraisal function established within an organization to examine and evaluate its activities as a service to the organization. The objective of internal auditing is to assist members of the organization in the effective discharge of their responsibilities. To this end, internal auditing furnishes them with analyses, appraisals, recommendations, counsel, and information concerning the activities reviewed. The audit objective includes promoting effective control at reasonable cost. (Introduction)

Internal Auditing Department includes any unit or activity within an organization which performs internal auditing functions.

Internal Auditor is an individual within an organization's internal auditing department who is assigned the responsibility of performing internal auditing functions.

Internal Control is a process within an organization designed to provide reasonable assurance regarding the achievement of the following primary objectives:

- The reliability and integrity of information.
- Compliance with policies, plans, procedures, laws, regulations, and contracts.
- The safeguarding of assets.
- The economical and efficient use of resources.
- The accomplishment of established objectives and goals for operations or programs. (300.05)

Irregularity refers to the intentional misstatement or omission of significant information in accounting records, financial statements, other reports, documents or records. Irregularities include (a) fraudulent financial reporting which renders financial statements misleading and (b) misappropriation of assets. Irregularities involve:

- Falsification or alteration of accounting or other records and supporting documents.
- Intentional misapplication of accounting principles.
- Misrepresentation or intentional omission of events, transactions, or other significant information. (280.01.1)

Management includes those individuals with responsibilities for setting and/or achieving the organization's objectives.

Monitoring encompasses supervising, observing, and testing activities and appropriately reporting to responsible individuals. Monitoring provides an ongoing verification of progress toward achievement of objectives and goals. (300.03.2b)

Objectives are the broadest statements of what the organization chooses to accomplish. (300.02.1)

Objectivity is an independent mental attitude which requires internal auditors to perform audits in such a manner that they have an honest belief in their work product and that no significant quality compromises are made. Objectivity requires internal auditors not to subordinate their judgment on audit matters to that of others. (120.01 and .02)

Operations refers to the recurring activities of an organization directed toward producing a product or rendering a service. Such activities may include, but are not limited to, marketing, sales, production, purchasing, human resources, finance and accounting, and governmental assistance. (350.01.1)

Outside Service Provider refers to a person or firm, independent of the organization, who has special knowledge, skill, and experience in a particular discipline. Outside service providers include, among others, actuaries, accountants, appraisers, environmental specialists, fraud investigators, lawyers, engineers, geologists, security specialists, statisticians, information technology specialists, the organization's external auditors, and other auditing organizations. An outside service provider may be engaged by the board, senior management, or the director of internal auditing.

Preventive Controls are actions taken to deter undesirable events from occurring. (300.06.1)

Proficiency means the ability to apply knowledge to situations likely to be encountered and to deal with them without extensive recourse to technical research and assistance. (250.01.1)

Programs refers to special purpose activities of an organization. Such activities include, but are not limited to, the raising of capital, sale of a facility, fund-raising campaigns, new product or service introduction campaigns, capital expenditures, and special purpose government grants. (350.01.2)

Purpose Statements in audit reports describe the audit objectives and may, where necessary, inform the reader why the audit was conducted and what it was expected to achieve. (430.04.3)

Quality Assurance is a program by which the director of internal auditing evaluates the operations of the internal auditing department. The purpose of the quality assurance program is to provide reasonable assurance that internal auditing work conforms with the *Standards for the Professional Practice of Internal Auditing*, the internal auditing department's charter, and other applicable standards. The quality assurance program should include the following elements:

- Supervision.
- Internal reviews.
- External reviews. (560.01)

Ratio Analysis is the study of financial condition and performance through ratios derived from items in the financial statements or from other financial or nonfinancial information. (420.01.1h)

Reasonableness Test is a comparison of an estimated amount, calculated by the use of relevant financial and nonfinancial information, with a recorded amount. (420.01.1h)

Recommendations are actions the internal auditor believes necessary to correct existing conditions or improve operations. (430.05.1)

Regression Analysis is a mathematical procedure which is used to determine and measure the predictive relationship between one variable (dependent variable) and one or more other variables (independent variable). (420.01.1h)

Risk is the probability that an event or action may adversely affect the organization or activity under audit. (410.01.1b and 520.04.2)

Risk Assessment is a systematic process for assessing and integrating professional judgments about probable adverse conditions and/or events. The risk assessment process should provide a means of organizing and integrating professional judgments for development of the audit work schedule. (520.04.10)

Risk Factors are the criteria used to identify the relative significance of, and likelihood that, conditions and/or events may occur that could adversely affect the organization. (520.04.6)

Scope Limitation is a restriction placed upon the internal auditing department that precludes the department from accomplishing its objectives and plans. Among other things, a scope limitation may restrict the:

- Scope defined in the charter.
- Department's access to records, personnel, and physical properties relevant to the performance of audits.
- Approved audit work schedule.
- Performance of necessary auditing procedures.
- Approved staffing plan and financial budget. (110.01.5b)

Senior Management refers to those individuals to whom the director of internal auditing is responsible.

Significant is the level of importance or magnitude assigned to an item, event, information, or problem by the internal auditor.

Significant Audit Findings are those conditions which, in the judgment of the director of internal auditing, could adversely affect the organization. Significant audit findings may include conditions dealing with irregularities, illegal acts, errors, inefficiency, waste, ineffectiveness, conflicts of interest, and control weaknesses. (110.01.6b)

Standards for the Professional Practice of Internal Auditing
(the *Standards*) are the criteria by which the operations of
an internal auditing department are evaluated and measured.
They are intended to represent the practice of internal auditing as it should be.

Statement of Responsibilities of Internal Auditing is a document which presents in summary form the:

• Objective and scope of internal auditing.
• Responsibility and authority of the internal auditing
  department.
• Independence of internal auditors.

Supervision is a process which begins with planning and continues throughout the examination, evaluation, report, and
follow-up phases of the audit assignment. Supervision includes:

• Ensuring that the auditors assigned possess the requi-
  site knowledge and skills.
• Providing appropriate instructions during the planning
  of the audit and approving the audit program.
• Seeing that the approved audit program is carried out
  unless changes are both justified and authorized.
• Determining that audit working papers adequately support the audit findings, conclusions, and reports.
• Ensuring that audit reports are accurate, objective, clear,
  concise, constructive, and timely.
• Ensuring that audit objectives are met
• Providing opportunities for developing internal auditors'
  knowledge and skills. (230.01 and .02)

Survey is a process for gathering information, without detailed verification, on the activity being examined. The main purposes are to:

- Understand the activity under review.
- Identify significant areas warranting special emphasis.
- Obtain information for use in performing the audit.
- Determine whether further auditing is necessary. (410.01.5a)

System (process, operation, function, or activity) is an arrangement, a set, or a collection of concepts, parts, activities, and/or people that are connected or interrelated to achieve objectives and goals. (This definition applies to both manual and automated systems.) A system may also be a collection of subsystems operating together for a common objective or goal. (300.02.3)

Trend Analysis is the analysis of the changes in a given item of information over a period of time. (420.01.1h)

Understanding means the ability to apply broad knowledge to situations likely to be encountered, to recognize significant deviations, and to be able to carry out the research necessary to arrive at reasonable solutions. (250.01.3)

Statement of Responsibilities of Internal Auditing

The purpose of this statement is to provide in summary form a general understanding of the responsibilities of internal auditing. For more specific guidance, readers should refer to the *Standards for the Professional Practice of Internal Auditing.*

OBJECTIVE AND SCOPE

Internal auditing is an independent appraisal function established within an organization to examine and evaluate its activities as a service to the organization. The objective of internal auditing is to assist members of the organization in the effective discharge of their responsibilities. To this end, internal auditing furnishes them with analyses, appraisals, recommendations, counsel, and information concerning the activities reviewed. The audit objective includes promoting effective control at reasonable cost. The members of the organization assisted by internal auditing include those in management and the board of directors.

The scope of internal auditing should encompass the examination and evaluation of the adequacy and effectiveness of the organization's system of internal control and the quality of performance in carrying out assigned responsibilities. Internal auditors should:

- Review the reliability and integrity of financial and operating information and the means used to identify, measure, classify, and report such information.
- Review the systems established to ensure compliance with those policies, plans, procedures, laws, regulations, and contracts which could have a significant impact on operations and reports, and should determine whether the organization is in compliance.
- Review the means of safeguarding assets and, as appropriate, verify the existence of such assets.

- Appraise the economy and efficiency with which resources are employed.
- Review operations or programs to ascertain whether results are consistent with established objectives and goals and whether the operations or programs are being carried out as planned.

RESPONSIBILITY AND AUTHORITY

The internal auditing department is an integral part of the organization and functions under the policies established by senior management and the board. The purpose, authority, and responsibility of the internal auditing department should be defined in a formal written document (charter). The director of internal auditing should seek approval of the charter by senior management as well as acceptance by the board. The charter should make clear the purposes of the internal auditing department, specify the unrestricted scope of its work, and declare that auditors are to have no authority or responsibility for the activities they audit.

Throughout the world internal auditing is performed in diverse environments and within organizations which vary in purpose, size, and structure. In addition, the laws and customs within various countries differ from one another. These differences may affect the practice of internal auditing in each environment. The implementation of the *Standards for the Professional Practice of Internal Auditing*, therefore, will be governed by the environment in which the internal auditing department carries out its assigned responsibilities. Compliance with the concepts enunciated by the *Standards for the Professional Practice of Internal Auditing* is essential before the responsibilities of internal auditors can be met. As stated in the *Code of Ethics*, Members of The Institute of Internal Auditors, Inc. and Certified Internal Auditors shall adopt suitable means to comply with the *Standards for the Professional Practice of Internal Auditing*.

INDEPENDENCE

Internal auditors should be independent of the activities they audit. Internal auditors are independent when they can carry out their work freely and objectively. Independence permits internal auditors to render the impartial and unbiased judgments essential to the proper conduct of audits. It is achieved through organizational status and objectivity.

The organizational status of the internal auditing department should be sufficient to permit the accomplishment of its audit responsibilities. The director of the internal auditing department should be responsible to an individual in the organization with sufficient authority to promote independence and to ensure a broad audit coverage, adequate consideration of audit reports, and appropriate action on audit recommendations.

Objectivity is an independent mental attitude which internal auditors should maintain in performing audits. Internal auditors are not to subordinate their judgment on audit matters to that of others. Designing, installing, and operating systems are not audit functions. Also, the drafting of procedures for systems is not an audit function. Performing such activities is presumed to impair audit objectivity.

The _Statement of Responsibilities of Internal Auditing_ was originally issued by The Institute of Internal Auditors in 1947. The current _Statement_, revised in 1990, embodies the concepts previously established and includes such changes as are deemed advisable in light of the present status of the profession.

The Institute of Internal Auditors *Code of Ethics*

PURPOSE: A distinguishing mark of a profession is acceptance by its members of responsibility to the interests of those it serves. Members of The Institute of Internal Auditors (Members) and Certified Internal Auditors (CIAs) must maintain high standards of conduct in order to effectively discharge this responsibility. The Institute of Internal Auditors (Institute) adopts this *Code of Ethics* for Members and CIAs.

APPLICABILITY: This *Code of Ethics* is applicable to all Members and CIAs. Membership in The Institute and acceptance of the "Certified Internal Auditor" designation are voluntary actions. By acceptance, Members and CIAs assume an obligation of self-discipline above and beyond the requirements of laws and regulations.

The standards of conduct set forth in this *Code of Ethics* provide basic principles in the practice of internal auditing. Members and CIAs should realize that their individual judgment is required in the application of these principles.

CIAs shall use the "Certified Internal Auditor" designation with discretion and in a dignified manner, fully aware of what the designation denotes. The designation shall also be used in a manner consistent with all statutory requirements.

Members who are judged by the Board of Directors of The Institute to be in violation of the standards of conduct of the *Code of Ethics* shall be subject to forfeiture of their membership in The Institute. CIAs who are similarly judged also shall be subject to forfeiture of the "Certified Internal Auditor" designation.

STANDARDS OF CONDUCT

I. Members and CIAs shall exercise honesty, objectivity, and diligence in the performance of their duties and responsibilities.

II. Members and CIAs shall exhibit loyalty in all matters pertaining to the affairs of their organization or to whomever they may be rendering a service. However, Members and CIAs shall not knowingly be a party to any illegal or improper activity.

III. Members and CIAs shall not knowingly engage in acts or activities which are discreditable to the profession of internal auditing or to their organization.

IV. Members and CIAs shall refrain from entering into any activity which may be in conflict with the interest of their organization or which would prejudice their ability to carry out objectively their duties and responsibilities.

V. Members and CIAs shall not accept anything of value from an employee, client, customer, supplier, or business associate of their organization which would impair or be presumed to impair their professional judgment.

VI. Members and CIAs shall undertake only those services which they can reasonably expect to complete with professional competence.

VII. Members and CIAs shall adopt suitable means to comply with the *Standards for the Professional Practice of Internal Auditing.*

VIII. Members and CIAs shall be prudent in the use of information acquired in the course of their duties. They shall not use confidential information for any personal gain nor in any manner which would be contrary to law or detrimental to the welfare of their organization.

IX. Members and CIAs, when reporting on the results of their work, shall reveal all material facts known to them which, if not revealed, could either distort reports of operations under review or conceal unlawful practices.

   X. Members and CIAs shall continually strive for improvement in their proficiency, and in the effectiveness and quality of their service.

  XI. Members and CIAs, in the practice of their profession, shall be ever mindful of the obligation to maintain the high standards of competence, morality, and dignity promulgated by The Institute. Members shall abide by the *Bylaws* and uphold the objectives of The Institute.

Adopted by Board of Directors July 1988.

Translation or Adaptation of the *Standards for the Professional Practice of Internal Auditing* and Other Standards-Related Pronouncements (Administrative Directive No. 2)

Purpose

This section describes the administrative procedures for adapting the *Standards* and other Standards-related pronouncements (Standards Pronouncements) to audit environments throughout the world and/or for translating them into languages other than English.

Legal Basis

The Standards Pronouncements of The Institute of Internal Auditors (IIA), as defined in the *Framework for the Standards for the Professional Practice of Internal Auditing*, are copyrighted by The Institute of Internal Auditors, 249 Maitland Avenue, Altamonte Springs, Florida 32701-4201, USA, whether separately published or published in any of The IIA's publications. All rights reserved.

Under copyright laws and agreements, no part of any of these Standards Pronouncements may be reproduced, stored in a retrieval system, or transmitted in any form by any means — electronic, mechanical, photocopying, recording, or otherwise — without prior written permission of The IIA. Except as provided by separate agreement, permission to adapt or translate the Standards Pronouncements is granted solely by The IIA. Distribution of approved adaptations or translations are to be made under the direction of National Institutes or Chapters of The IIA.

Translation

Translation of The IIA's Standards Pronouncements into languages other than English is necessary to provide the same level of guidance to all Members of The IIA, National Institutes, Chapters, and Audit Clubs. Permission should be obtained from The IIA before any translations are initiated in order to obtain appropriate guidance and, where translations have already been approved, to avoid having unnecessary variations in the translations into any one language.

The IIA encourages National Institutes and Chapters where English is not the primary language to furnish translations of The IIA's Standards Pronouncements to their Members, provided that:

1. The translation is in a form as close as possible to, and preserves the concepts of, the original.

2. Copies of the translation submitted to The IIA are accompanied by a statement signed by the President of the National Institute or Chapter and by a qualified translator, attesting that the meanings and concepts of the original have been preserved.

3. Permission is obtained from The IIA before the translation is published.

4. To provide a minimum level of guidance, the translated Standards Pronouncements should include the *Statement of Responsibilities of Internal Auditing,* the *Code of Ethics,* and the General and Specific *Standards for the Professional Practice of Internal Auditing.*

5. The translated version includes a translated statement that "Permission has been obtained from the copyright holder, The Institute of Internal Auditors, 249 Maitland Avenue, Altamonte Springs, Florida 32701-4201, USA, to publish this translation, which is the same in all material respects, as the original."

Adaptation

Laws, regulations, and customs of different countries may require that Standards Pronouncements be adapted for use in the audit environments of such countries. Before publication of adapted Standards Pronouncements to their Members, National Institutes or Chapters are required to:

1. Apply to The IIA for approval of the adaptation, indicating the nature of any modifications, the reasons they are required, and the effect on the professional practice of internal auditing in the country if such modifications are not made.

2. Provide copies of the adapted and, where appropriate, translated documents to The IIA, accompanied by a statement attesting that, to the extent they are applicable to the local environment, the concepts contained in the original document have been preserved in the adaptation. Attestation statements must be signed by the President of the National Institute or Chapter and, for translated documents, by a qualified translator.

3. Include in all adapted versions the statement that "Permission has been obtained from the copyright holder, The Institute of Internal Auditors, 249 Maitland Avenue, Altamonte Springs, Florida 32701-4201, USA, to publish this adaptation of the original for use in (name of country). The concepts enunciated in the original have been preserved in this adapted version."

Proposing Changes or Additions to Standards Pronouncements

Nothing in this statement should preclude a National Institute or Chapter from proposing changes or additions to any of The IIA's Standards Pronouncements. Suggestions of this nature should be directed to the Chairman of the Internal Auditing Standards Board.

Acknowledgments

The Institute of Internal Auditors (IIA) is grateful to those governmental agencies, professional organizations, internal and external auditors, and members of management, boards of directors, and academe who provided guidance and assistance in the development and interpretation of the *Standards*, the *Statement of Responsibilities of Internal Auditing*, and the *Code of Ethics*. The IIA is deeply indebted to those individuals who served on the Internal Auditing Standards Board and its subcommittees through the years.

SUBCOMMITTEE ON CODIFICATION OF THE STANDARDS

Susan B. Lione, CIA

INTERNAL AUDITING STANDARDS BOARD 1996–1997

Wayne G. Moore, CIA, Chairman

Cheryl L. Aldeman, CIA
Armando Andrade, CIA
Andrew D. Bailey, PhD, CIA
Paul A. Bellamy, CIA
C.A. Davidson
Len L. Davis, CIA
Roland De Meulder
Kelly D. Graves, CIA
Edward J. Kain, CIA
Warren E. Malmquist, CIA
Sam M. McCall, CIA
Maria E. Mendes, CIA
Steven S. Mezzio, CIA
Robert Pawelski, CIA

PRACTICES CENTER

Basil H. Pflumm, CIA, Vice President
Susan B. Lione, CIA, Manager
Lucy Sheets, Coordinator